Education Improvement
For The Disadvantaged
In An Elementary Setting

Education Improvement
For The Disadvantaged
In An Elementary Setting

By

GORDON P. LIDDLE, Ph.D.

*Director, Interprofessional Research Commission
on Pupil Personnel Services
Lecturer, College of Education
University of Maryland
College Park, Maryland*

ROBERT E. ROCKWELL, M.S.

*Coordinator, Preschool Readiness Centers
Southern Illinois University
Center for the Study of Crime, Delinquency and Corrections
East St. Louis, Illinois*

EVELYN SACADAT, B.A.

*Director, Project Head Start
Board of Education
Quincy, Illinois*

CHARLES C THOMAS • PUBLISHER
Springfield • Illinois • U.S.A.

Published and Distributed Throughout the World by
CHARLES C THOMAS • PUBLISHER
BANNERSTONE HOUSE
301-327 East Lawrence Avenue, Springfield, Illinois, U.S.A.
NATCHEZ PLANTATION HOUSE
735 North Atlantic Boulevard, Fort Lauderdale, Florida, U.S.A.

Library of Congress Catalog Card Number: 67-18342

With THOMAS BOOKS *careful attention is given to all details of manufacturing and design. It is the Publisher's desire to present books that are satisfactory as to their physical qualities and artistic possibilities and appropriate for their particular use.* THOMAS BOOKS *will be true to those laws of quality that assure a good name and good will.*

This research was supported in its entirety by
U.S. PUBLIC HEALTH SERVICE
NATIONAL INSTITUTE OF MENTAL HEALTH
GRANT MH 0633

PREFACE

T HIS REPORT is an attempt to help the reader profit from the experiences of a group of educators who attempted over a period of five years to aid a community in doing a better job of educating the children of the poor in the kindergarten-primary grades. The program had two principal thrusts: one, an attempt to involve the parents of disadvantaged children in the education of their children through a number of means, principally home visits and parent meetings; and two, an attempt to provide disadvantaged children with an enriched environment both during the school day and in the after-school and summer hours through assistance to teachers and the extensive use of adolescent and adult volunteers.

The final section of the report summarizes the research findings, discusses the impact of the project upon the school system and the community, and points to the implications of this effort for other communities who have a concern for disadvantaged youth, and for those who hope to bring about changes in the education of the children of the poor.

The staff wishes to acknowledge the encouragement and moral support of its two godfathers, Robert J. Havighurst of the University of Chicago and William Hollister of the University of North Carolina.

Five additional persons should also be recognized: our colleague, Alan Lentz, who spent two years working with parents and teachers; Dr. Randall McClelland, Chairman

v

of the Quincy Youth Development Commission; Rolland
W. McFarland, its Treasurer; Walter Blunt, Chairman of
the School's Advisory Committee; and Ruth Porter, who
performed many roles, from typist to volunteer.

GORDON P. LIDDLE
ROBERT E. ROCKWELL
EVELYN SACADAT

CONTENTS

TABLES

Education Improvement
For The Disadvantaged
In An Elementary Setting

Chapter I

BACKGROUND AND ORGANIZATION
OF THE PROJECT

The Community

M ORE THAN a century ago Lincoln and Douglas debated in Illinois' second largest city, Quincy. The first settlers were new Englanders. The railroad brought the Irish, and political unrest in Germany brought the largest ethnic group, the Germans—both Catholic and Protestant. For a time the city grew rapidly, but with the decline of the Mississippi packets it became relatively isolated from metropolitan areas. Today's population of 45,000 is only 15 per cent greater than it was sixty years ago. Like many small cities in the midwestern farm belt, conservative political and economic thinking predominates. More than 30 per cent of the children attend parochial schools. About three per cent of the population is Negro.

Between 30 and 35 per cent of the community's children fail to finish high school, while from 20 to 25 per cent begin college. The large Catholic population and the city's industrial wealth allow the community to run an average school system with the lowest school tax rate among the thirty downstate cities. The per pupil expenditure for education is about average for Illinois.

In this type of community there is less social mobility than in a rapidly growing urban area. The area of town a child comes from, the house he lives in, and his parent's

3

occupation are all rather well known and profoundly affect the community's educational expectations for him. When the potential high school graduating class of 1958 was divided into four social class levels based upon these criteria, it was found that 76 per cent of the children in the upper middle class went on to college, along with 2 per cent of those in the lowest social class level, a group comprising the bottom 28 per cent of the population. The corresponding percentages of dropouts from these two groups were 5 per cent and 66 per cent respectively.

Reasons for Initiation of This Study

While the education of the culturally disadvantaged has become a national concern in recent years, this project began in a more personal way. In 1951, a group of social scientists from the University of Chicago moved to Qunicy to experiment with methods of helping the city prevent maladjustment and develop the talents of its children. This group, headed by Robert J. Havighurst and Paul Bowman, had been rather successful in establishing meaningful programs for gifted children and in establishing and strengthening community agencies for emotionally disturbed children, but many children from lower-class families continued to do poorly in school.

Thirteen public elementary schools and two Protestant parochial schools send their children to a centrally located junior high and to a single senior high school. The graduates of four of these elementary schools did very poorly in the city-wide secondary schools. Among the potential high school graduating classes of 1958 and 1960, only 47 per cent of the graduates of these schools finished high school, and only 9 per cent, mostly athletes, began college. In the ninth grade their graduates received more D's and F's than A's in academic subjects.

Among the minority who finished high school, few did well academically and socially many were unhappy. Approximately 59 per cent of the city's delinquents attended these four schools, more than twice their "fair share." Interviews with employers and marriage ratings indicated other trouble areas. Clearly there was a need to modify the educational experience of children attending these schools.*

The first effort was directed at nonachieving secondary school students. In 1955, the senior author and the public schools began a program for "slow learners" in the secondary schools.† Curricular modifications and group guidance experiences were developed in the hope of better meeting the needs of this group. An initial evaluation in 1957 indicated that the program enabled its participants to have a more positive view of themselves and society and was moderately effective in reducing delinquent behavior. But the program had little or no effect upon academic achievement. Further data collected in 1961 and again in 1965 indicated that there were no significant differences in the marriage ratings or work adjustment of the experimental as compared to the control group in the slow learner study. The general evaluation of this effort can probably be summed up in the phrase, "too little and too late."

The successes and failures with the secondary program led the senior author to attempt a pilot program during the 1957-59 years in the primary grades at Whitman School.** Here the principal and several teachers had expressed an interest in experimenting with remedial methods in the

---

*Havighurst, Robert J., *et al.*: *Mobilizing Community Resources for Youth.* Univ. of Chicago, 1956.

†An experimental program for slow learning adolescents. *Educational Leadership*, December, 1965.

**Experimental room for slow learners in the primary grades. *Elementary School Journal*, April, 1958.

primary grades. In the fall of 1957, a classroom was established for fifteen children who had been unsuccessful the previous year in the first grade. Home visits by the teacher, help in setting up field trips, more easy reading books, and fewer children in the classroom led a number of the previously unsuccessful children to increase their learning rate, some spectacularly.

However, during the next two years the number of children in the class was gradually raised to eighteen, then to twenty, and finally to twenty-three. The experimental teacher began to say, "Why teach twenty-three children with severe learning problems when the other second grade teacher has only twenty-seven average and above average children?" When the principal was transferred to a middle-class school, the teacher reluctantly decided to move to an easier assignment in a middle-class school. Frequently this is the history of experimentation and return to the status quo in school systems. Nevertheless, the subsequent achievement of the children in this pilot program led to the decision to initiate the present action research.

Aims of the Program

The objectives of the program as spelled out in the original proposal were as follows:

1. To understand the child more fully through information obtained by testing, interviewing parents, and observing children.
2. To provide a richer background of intellectually stimulating experiences for the child through a better use of community resources and school facilities and materials.
3. To enlist the interest, support, and cooperation of the parents in helping to motivate the child to develop his interests and abilities.

The Schools

All four project schools lie close to the Mississippi, the first section of the city to be settled. In this century there has been almost no new residential building in any of these areas except for the low cost apartments built by the Federal government during the depression. After World War II, the suburban areas surrounding the city began to grow, and all of the "river wards" and their schools began to lose population. The schools, all built before 1930, are in a good state of repair. Except in suburban areas their equipment would probably be considered typical. Closed circuit television, school libraries, science labs, provisions for showing films in the classroom, teaching machines, and similar modern teaching aids are neither found nor expected here, but buildings are well lighted, uncrowded, clean, and painted. These are not the schools of "blackboard jungle." There are no bars on the windows, police or threatening signs in the hallways, rats in the basement, or other signs of advanced decay sometimes found in urban slum schools.

The Teachers

In any action research program, the experimenter is faced with deciding whether to work with an unselected sample of teachers, ask for volunteers, or carefully select outstanding teachers who are enthusiastic about the experiment. These latter groups are usually already well above the average in competency and teaching effectiveness, and thus can almost surely guarantee favorable results, but results which cannot be duplicated on a massive basis. In New York City, for example, it is not surprising that the

Higher Horizons program with thirty-five dollars a year extra to spend and "run of the mine" teachers has been unable to duplicate the effectiveness of its pilot program which worked in one junior high district with an enthusiastic staff and three hundred dollars a year extra to spend.

In this program it was decided to work with an unselected sample of teachers. This reduced the novelty and effectiveness of the program, but increased its applicability to other school systems. In almost every case the control and experimental children had the same teachers.

Nationwide, the teachers of the poor are below average in their formal training. They come from a different socioeconomic strata than the children they teach, and only rarely have they had any training to prepare them to overcome the learning difficulties of culturally disadvantaged children. As a consequence, teachers in slum areas are frequently discouraged. A majority, once they have seniority, apply for transfers to teach the children they were taught to teach, the children of the middle class. Some teachers choose to remain in these schools because the need is great, but others remain because not too much is expected of them. We found that evening meetings and after-school sessions were distasteful to some teachers who were accustomed to leaving school as soon as possible after dismissal.

Most of the project teachers and principals were trained at nearby teachers' colleges. A majority grew up in the city or in nearby rural communities. They were attracted by the city's cultural and shopping advantages. They looked upon the city as a desirable place to live. Teachers in this system generally did not visit other schools and did not attend professional meetings outside the county. More than three-fourths of the project teachers had taught in their school for more than four years, a number for more than twenty-five years.

Experimental Design

The study population consisted of two groups. The control group included all children who attended kindergarten classes in the four experimental schools in 1960-61, plus those children who joined this group during the first half of the first grade in 1961-62. This group numbered 227. Of this group 162, or 71 per cent were still available for testing in the public schools at the conclusion of the study. An additional 7 per cent transferred to Catholic schools at the end of kindergarten and were not retested. Since the project didn't actually get a staff until January 1961, a few pupils who should have been in this group moved before they were tested or even recorded as members of the group.

The experimental group entered kindergarten in the fall of 1961, one year later than the control group. This group was also kept open until the middle of the first grade. Of this group, 135 of the total of 229, or 59 per cent, were available for post testing. This was a smaller percentage than was available in the control group for two reasons. First, as was explained, some students who should have been in the control group moved too soon to be included. Secondly, sixteen experimental children entered kindergarten but moved before even the initial tests were given.

During the second semester of kindergarten each child in the experimental and control group was given at least two measures of intellectual functioning—the Wechsler Intelligence Scale for Children (WISC) and the Peabody Picture Vocabulary Test. All tests for both groups were individually administered by the same psychological examiner. The WISC and Peabody were readministered during the last two months of the third grade, approximately four years later, so that changes in the intellectual growth of the experimental and control groups could be measured.

In addition, each year the attendance of each child was recorded. Teacher administered tests such as the Metropolitan Reading Readiness Test, the Primary Mental Abilities Test, and certain of the Iowa achievement tests were recorded for comparison purposes. Teachers of kindergarten and first grade children were asked to nominate certain of their children as headed for success or failure in school. In the third grade a self-concept instrument was also administered for comparison purposes. These tests will be discussed more fully in the chapter on results, Chapter VI.

Since the staff was interested in finding out what types of children seemed to have been helped by the project, certain other data were recorded for later analysis. The following are examples of data which allowed analysis of subgroupings of children: the degree of cultural disadvantage of the child as measured by home interviews, the education of the parents, and the scores of children who had siblings in the comparison group.

Basically then, the project staff proposed to study one group as it passed from kindergarten through the primary grades and to compare this group at the end of the third grade with the next group to enter kindergarten, the experimental group. The investigators hoped to improve the life experiences of the second group through curricular modifications, work with the parents, and after-school and summer experiences utilizing volunteers.

The Staff

The composition of the staff varied from year to year.

It averaged about two and a half professional persons and a secretary who worked three-fourths time. Except for the principal investigator, an educational psychologist who devoted half-time to the project, all staff members were recruited from the local community. The initial testing was done by a psychometrist who had no other duties. The other staff members were a social worker and several persons who were teaching in the local schools. These former teachers and social worker were usually referred to as "family workers," because this was the most distinctive of their roles, but they all worked with parents, volunteers, and children. Some family workers spent a greater percentage of their time working with parents than did others. The range varied from 15 per cent to 40 per cent. Similar ranges were typical in working with teachers, children, and volunteers. Each staff member had major responsibility for work with particular classes in one or two of the schools, but the staff generally functioned as a team with only moderate differentiation of function.

The project represents about 11.5 years of professional staff time which could be broken down in the following manner:

Staff Time Devoted to	Percentage of Time	Staff Years
Administration	7.6	.9
Testing	18.4	2.1
Research and writeup	14.0	1.6
Work with children	22.0	2.5
Work with parents	22.0	2.3
Work with volunteers	9.8	1.1
Work with teachers	8.2	.9

Roughly 60 per cent of the staff's time was devoted directly to the action phase of the project while the other 40 per cent was devoted to testing, research, and administration. One professional person could handle about four classrooms if he were not responsible for administration of funds, testing, and research.

Chapter II

THE INITIAL PHASES
OF THE EXPERIMENT

Perhaps the project's first important decision was that all of the children would be worked with in the experimental groups in the four schools. The percentage of culturally disadvantaged children in these schools was so high, and the percentage of their graduates who really did well in secondary school was so low, that probably almost any child growing up in the neighborhood was to a degree disadvantaged. Since raising teachers' and parents' expectations for these children was one of the aims of the project, it was thought inadvisable to segregate the children of the less adequate families by using a track system or ability grouping.

This decision and other basic decisions were made by an advisory committee of teachers, principals, and central office school administrators appointed by the superintendent to work with the principal investigator. The committee included the principal and one teacher from each of the four schools, a school social worker, the school psychologist, the elementary supervisor, the assistant superintendent for curriculum and several principals from other schools in the system. The group met twice a month for about three months to discuss what educational modifications were needed for the disadvantaged. They discussed the possibility of experimenting with the ungraded primary, or of having children remain with one teacher for more than one year, and also the possibility of experimenting with individualized reading.

While attendance at committee meetings was good and interest seemed high, it was found that the commitee was too large and its authority too unclear for the group to take effective action. The project director made suggestions that certain modifications such as individualized reading or an ungraded primary be tried, but generally these decisions were in turn referred to the principals of the four schools. These men were sometimes moderately interested in trying certain of the possible modifications but only if their teachers were interested. The teachers, in turn, felt that any major modifications would have to have the blessing of the central office administrators. Basically, despite the evidences of the serious shortcomings of the present program, school people felt that if only the parents would take an interest in their children, and if teachers would work a little harder using the methods they were presently using, the desired results could be obtained.

To be perfectly frank, at this point the principal investigator almost decided to give up the experiment. In part, time itself was to blame. Originally, it was planned to have a full year to test the control group and to plan the action program, but the money became available at mid-year. To avoid losing an entire year, the testing and planning were compressed into the second semester. Subsequently, parts of the project which did not require basic changes in school organization or curriculum were conceived and blossomed, but major curriculum modifications were never attempted. It was never clear to the experimental teachers to whom they should be looking for curriculum leadership.

While in subsequent years a smaller working committee

composed of the director, the four principals, and two central office persons met occasionally, this initial lack of clarity of decision as to what curriculum modifications were to be tried made the project largely ineffective in this area. In subsequent years, the working committee confined itself largely to seeing to it that project staff and volunteers worked smoothly with project teachers and that the necessary research data was collected. Occasionally it planned meetings with project teachers to train them to do parent interviews, to evaluate the year's work, or to orient the next year's experimental teachers; but its evaluation of the project was not systematic, and it made no formal reports to the school administration or to the Board.

The June Kindergarten

Perhaps the most significant curricular modification agreed upon by the advisory committee was the decision to have each child come to school for one week in the June prior to his entrance into kindergarten. More than three-fourths of the children who entered kindergarten in the fall of 1961 took advantage of the opportunity to meet with their teacher and five or six of their classmates for a week in June. Each teacher met with one group in the morning and another in the afternoon each week until all her prospective students had had their turn.

During the week parents were encouraged to meet with the teacher, so the teacher had the opportunity to meet most of the parents and to get to know the children rather well. In the small group children became familiar with their teacher, the school, and its routine in a quiet, relaxed atmosphere. This made it possible for both teacher and pupils to get off to a good start in the fall. Project funds were used to pay the teachers; in subsequent years the School Board has supported the continuation of the June kindergarten in all of these schools.

Initial Home Interviews

One of the purposes of the June kindergarten was to begin the work with families as early as possible. The project staff supplemented by principals hired with project funds began to interview the experimental and control group parents in their homes. These initial interviews were used to get acquainted with the parents and to collect information on the child's degree of cultural handicap.

We thought of cultural handicap in terms of the presence or absence of the opportunities and advantages normally available to a majority of American youngsters, advantages which seem necessary if the child is to make satisfactory progress in a typical school. Therefore, information was collected on the child's experiences with books, music, paints, travel, mealtime conversation, and household routines. The interviewer also collected information about the parent's own interests, education, and job, and about the parent's hopes and expectations for his child.

Despite the tendency for most people to place themselves in a favorable light and to tell the interviewer what they think he wants to hear, less than one-fourth of the experimental parents indicated that they had finished high school. Only nine of 748 parents in families interviewed, or 1.2 per cent, indicated that they had graduated from college. Eight of the nine were in the control group. An additional 4.5 per cent of each group indicated that they had had some education beyond high school, most a semester or two of college.

Seventy-eight per cent of the mothers and 76 per cent of the fathers in the experimental families indicated that they did not finish high school. The comparable figures for the control group were 63 per cent and 66 per cent respectively. A chi-square test of these differences indicated at the 1 per cent level of confidence that the control group mothers were better educated than the experimental mothers; the significance level for fathers was the 5 per cent level.

On the basis of the initial interviews the project staff rated about 45 per cent of the families as quite handicapping and about 30 per cent as moderately so. The remaining 25 per cent of the families were judged to be average or above average in this respect.

On a verbal level, the parental ambitions for their children were rather high, but often the child-rearing practices did not further these ambitions. Many parents mentioned that they hoped their children would go to college. Most of the rest indicated that they wanted their children to go "all the way"; that is, finish high school. Nevertheless about 80 per cent indicated that they did no serious reading themselves and three-fourths had never taken their children to the public library which is located in this section of the city. Forty per cent of the children eat breakfast either alone or with their siblings only. This was regarded as an indication that mealtime conversation probably does not provide much intellectual stimulation in these families.

Except for church there were very few families which had any contact with voluntary educational, cultural, civic, or philanthropic organizations. According to the parents about half of the children had more than occasional contact with a Sunday School or church, but a previous study of dropouts in Quincy found that 64 per cent were unknown to any minister or priest, so this figure is probably colored by the desire to be socially acceptable. Most of the churched families were served by a pentecostal Baptist church and the Assembly of God. Less than 3 per cent of the families were connected to the six most prestigious churches in town, although several of these churches are located in the river wards.

More than 85 per cent of the parents grew up within 100 miles of Quincy; about half in the city and the rest in hamlets or on farms. Many of the parents from rural backgrounds volunteered that they would be glad to return to the farm if they could make a living there. They don't care much for living in town and often visit relatives in rural Missouri in the summer or on weekends.

The parents' lack of education has restricted their employment largely to semiskilled and unskilled labor.

Initial Comparison of Experimental and Control Groups

Perhaps it is not surprising therefore, that the initial intelligence testing indicated that, on the average, both experimental and control group children had below average measured intelligence, and that the experimental group scored somewhat lower on all intellectual measures than did the control group. Table I indicates these results.

TABLE I
INITIAL INTELLIGENCE TEST RESULTS

Test	Mean		Std Deviation		Critical Ratio	Level of Significance
	X	C	X	C		
Weschler (WISC)						
Verbal	90.1	92.6	13.7	13.5	1.59	N.S.
Performance	94.7	98.2	15.3	15.5	1.97	5%
Total	91.6	94.7	14.7	14.4	1.71	N.S.
Peabody Picture						
Vocabulary	91.7	97.8	18.6	15.4	3.02	1%

It would seem that the control group had significantly higher measured intellectual ability at the beginning of the study. Table II would seem to indicate that the two groups did not differ significantly in the degree of cultural handicap as measured by the home interviews.

TABLE II

DEGREE OF CULTURAL HANDICAP

Amount of Handicap

Group	Considerable	Moderate	Little or None	Total	Chi-square
Experimental	94	60	55	209	
					.56 not sig.
Control	88	57	61	206	

The final early comparison of the two groups was the Metropolitan Test of Reading Readiness administered by the classroom teachers near the end of the kindergarten. These results would seem to indicate that the experimental group's lower initial reading readiness was not statistically significant.

TABLE III

METROPOLITAN TEST OF READING READINESS

Reading Readiness Rating (Cumulative Percentage)

Group	Very Low	Low	Low Avg.	Avg.	High Avg.	High	Very High	Chi-Square
Experimental	17	31	46	49	71	85	100	
								2.81 not significant
Control	16	28	38	56	62	84	100	

Thus the initial testing and interviewing would seem to indicate that the two groups were, on the average, not greatly different, but that the control group came from somewhat better educated families and had higher initial scores on the intellectual measures.

Chapter III

CURRICULAR MODIFICATIONS
AND ENRICHMENT EXPERIENCES

T HIS CHAPTER will describe the efforts of the project staff
to enrich the school experience of the experimental children
and their after-school and summer hours. An activity which
is new and enriching in one school system may be regarded
as commonplace in another; some of the teachers' and staff's
innovations may seem to be only good teaching to the
reader. Some of the enrichment experiences were designed
to furnish children with skills which in other communities
schools can reasonably assume that children have when they
enter school. Other activities should be part of the life
experience of all American children, but are rare in even
upper-middle-class communities and homes.

Field Trips

Field trips are a very economical means of providing
enrichment experiences. The basic objective of the field
trip is to provide understanding through experience. During
the four project years the teachers and staff conducted over
100 field trips to forty different sites. Previously, teachers
had taken children on one or two field trips a year. During
the project the typical number was eight to ten a year.

The curriculum was often built around field trip experiences. Teachers found that preparation for, and follow
up of field trips, greatly increased their educational value.

Plans for the trip appeared on experience charts, "Where Are We Going?" "How are We Going?" "What Questions Do We Already Have?" "What do We Want to Ask About While We Are There?"

After the trip, the teacher tried to reinforce children's learnings. She used a number of methods. Often she began by trying to discover what knowledge and attitudes resulted from the trip. "How often can a mother pony have a baby?" "What do ponies eat?" "Would you want to work in an apple orchard?" "What kinds of jobs did the farmer have to do every morning?"

On returning to the classroom, children drew pictures of what they had seen. Usually words were written under these pictures which told about aspects of the trip which were of significance to a given child. Sometimes pictures were glued together as a scroll and run through an old TV cabinet; the class produced its own TV show. Experience charts, posters, displays, and original stories followed the trip. When stories or thank-you letters were written in language class, an effort was made to have children highlight the incidents which were important to them. Polaroid pictures were fitted with captions suggested by the children and placed on the bulletin board. They served to help children remember significant aspects of their experiences and aided in discussion of the trip at a later date.

Field trips don't have to be to distant places to have educational value. Many of the best trips were within walking distance, most others within three miles of school. A child may pass a garage every day on his way to school or be dragged through a supermarket every Friday and still learn a great deal from a guided tour of one of these establishments, especially if someone has briefed the institutional guide so that he can show the children interesting aspects of his work using language they can understand.

Despite children's almost universal love of field trips and teachers' recognition of their educational value, most teachers take very few trips. It is much easier to stay in the classroom and stick to the text. The teacher who wants to take a trip typically has to make her own arrangements. She must call the farm or factory to get permission to come and also justify the trip to her principal. A planning session with the institutional guide is almost essential, and this must be done after school. Next the teacher must duplicate and send home permission slips and follow up on those children who don't return them. If the school doesn't provide buses, there is money to collect. At this point the teacher is free to begin worrying about children's safety as they cross streets and her financial liability if someone is injured. Perhaps it is not surprising that most teachers lack the initiative, energy, time, and money to take many trips.

The project staff and the parents were able to make it relatively easy to take trips. Together, staff and teachers planned the objectives, and the pre- and post-trip activities. The staff did the telephoning to arrange the trip and planned the itinerary with the guide. Unreturned permission slips were excuses for a home visit, so no one was left behind.

Since the school's budget for buses was very limited, most trips were taken using teacher, staff, and parent automobiles—no money to collect. On the trip the family worker and several parents he had recruited made safety less of a problem. In addition, having a number of adults along gives children an opportunity to do more talking and questioning. Parental participation demonstrated to the children their parents' interest in their schooling, and gave the parents a chance to see how the teacher capitalized on informal learning opportunities.

When a child's father worked at a place being visited, whether it was the city park, the fire station, the dairy, or airport, an attempt was made to have him serve as the group's guide. The world of work doesn't usually have much glamour in these neighborhoods; we thought that the trips helped make work seem important.

Finally, the staff secured the library materials, the film strips, films, records, charts, pictures, and samples which the teacher needed to develop the educational potentials of the trip.

Extensive planning among the teachers and project staff enabled field trip experiences to cover almost every subject matter being taught. A summary chart for the various schools was kept to prevent unnecessary duplication of trips.

A social studies unit on transportation and a science unit on the preservation of food provided an excellent opportunity for a double-barrelled field trip. Only two students had ever ridden on a train, and what child doesn't want to? With the aid of the worker, the teacher and students planned a bus and train trip to a chicken processing plant forty miles away. Many skills were developed, including map reading to find the way and arithmetic to figure the cost of the tickets; later, thank-you letters were written to the canning company, and stories telling about the trip were included in a parent newsletter.

The school system provided a bus for the first leg of the journey and the narration by a company salesman encouraged many questions. After light refreshments furnished by the company, it was "off to the railroad station." The quaint old small town station gave the students a glimpse of the past, as under the teacher's direction they compared it with the modern city station. The streamliner had to be flagged down. The children were thrilled to ride in the observation car, give the conductor their own tickets, see the kitchen and dining cars, and of course visit the restrooms, all for fifty-six cents. Although some had to make time payments, every student provided his own money.

Most of the places the children visited are available in every community—a bank, bakery, florist's shop, construction site, restaurant, lumber yard, and shoe store, to name only a few.

Developing Listening Skills

Underprivileged children live in crowded neighborhoods and crowded apartments. They are assaulted by auditory stimuli. Babies and parents yell, the neighbors fight, horns blow, and the television blares, but many of these sounds have little positive meaning for the child, and he learns to shut out many of the sounds around him, including the voices of teachers.

To combat this, the children were exposed to a program designed to help them become more careful listeners. Distinctive sounds ranging from cowbells and typewriters to jack hammers were played accompanied by visual stimuli. Later, almost all children could identify all of the sounds correctly without visual cues.

Moving from this, listening exercises were developed by presenting the instruments of the orchestra in the same manner. Trips to hear the elementary school band also helped. Once the children were able to identify the instruments by sound alone, a music bee was held. In order to help your team win you had to be able to identify the instrument on a short selection from a record. Under these circumstances first and second graders listened carefully, a characteristic which added to their enjoyment of the symphony concerts they began to attend.

Puppetry

Culturally disadvantaged children usually have verbal difficulties and tend to have a more physical pattern of communication. For this reason we capitalized on role-playing situations. In discussions which followed role-playing experiences, the children were often quite articulate. They enjoyed talking about the scenes they had acted out or had seen acted out by their classmates.

We found that puppetry could also be used to increase verbal expression. Original stories, usually ones with lots of violence, and such children's favorites as "Make Way for Ducklings," "The Three Wishes," and "Little Red Riding Hood" were acted out using puppets which the children made of materials such as plastic foam decorated with magic marker pens or socks with sewn-on button faces.

One class decided to put on a show for their parents. They designed and painted scenery, made handbills, and painted a puppet stage. The large crowd at the parent meeting was so enthusiastic that it was decided to "take the show on the road." The children performed at all four schools for their age mates and also at a PTA meeting.

These shows forced the children to organize their ideas sequentially and in some instances increased children's speaking vocabulary. The success of the first show led other schools to follow suit. Teachers encouraged their students to choose stories from their reading classes, elect characters, memorize parts, and present their shows for parent groups and other children in their schools. The puppets served to foster a broader development of oral communication by project children and provided many children with a success experience.

Science Classes

A staff member organized science classes at Langley School in one first grade class. Each child attended for a half hour twice a week while the teacher taught reading to the other half of the class. Simple scientific experiments having to do with color-mixing, evaporation, fire, expansion of gasses, seed-growing, and similar experiments stimulated children's thinking regarding their immediate environment. The instructor attempted to get students to ask questions and to find answers through observation and experiment rather than lecture. Robert Hess' experiments with young children and their mothers would seem to indicate that the amount of child talk during a learning situation is significantly related to the rate of student learning, while the amount of teacher talk is not. No attempt was made to measure the results, but the pupils enjoyed running the experiments and talking about them.

Language Classes

At the beginning of the third grade, the social studies unit included a study of Mexico. A staff consultant who was versed in the language started a class in spoken Spanish at Ross School for one-half hour before school twice a week. Attendance was usually 100 per cent. From this class two programs evolved: one was a Mexican Christmas Fiesta; the other, plays and conversations to demonstrate the many skills in speaking and singing which the children had learned. Parents were involved through making very simple crepe paper costumes for both programs. Attendance at these parent meetings was almost 100 per cent.

At Langley School a college volunteer conducted French classes which were held during the regular school day. The enthusiasm of third graders was evidenced when they gave a program for parents.

Library

To combat the problem of lack of interest in reading at an early stage, the local library was used extensively. In the kindergarten year the children were introduced to the library. This was done during classroom time by taking the children on walking excursions to the library to look around the children's department. They were given the opportunity to watch puppet shows presented by the department staff. This staff projected a warmth and interest to the children which continually reinforced the joys of reading.

During the first grade the same procedure was followed. In addition, each child in the project was given a library card. Staff members and classroom teachers encouraged use of library facilities. During the summer months, in conjunction with the summer reading program, the children were taken to the library or to the bookmobile once weekly by their teachers.

During the second grade the Girl Scout library project was started; it is described in a later chapter. This program emphasized regular trips to the library and served to get many of the children into the library habit. College students volunteered to work with the students on Saturdays and after school. These students provided the children with continued exposure to the library and its facilities.

In order to acquaint the parents with the library and its staff, a four-school parent group meeting was held at the building, as described in Chapter IV. It served to make the line of communication between the home and the library less formal and thereby more effective.

Films

The Quincy Public School System has an excellent film library, and it was utilized continually by the teachers. Use was made of films from the Public Health Department, the Illinois Bell Telephone, the public library, the local airlines, the local rail and truck lines. All were able to supply good, up-to-date, colorful materials which served to complement field trips and enrichment experiences.

Magazines for Class and Home

Many of our children had almost no reading material at home and no pictures to look at. Postal regulations allow qualified groups to have access to current issues of undeliverable magazines. These current magazines were picked up on a bimonthly basis and were put to use in the classroom. Children cut out pictures of modes of transportation or types of food, for example, or the teacher cut out pictures and asked the children to group together those pictures which one might expect to find in a department store, or all objects related to preparing food. After a time each child was able to choose a magazine to take home if he liked. Many individuals were very willing to donate their recent picture magazines to the project.

Pets

Small, crowded apartments and overburdened working mothers frequently cut these children off from contact with pets. While teachers thought it valuable to give the children the experience of feeding and caring for a variety of pets, they didn't want to turn the classroom into a zoo, nor did they want to care for the animals indefinitely. Therefore the staff secured a large cage for each classroom and moved various animals from room to room. After animals had been rotated through the rooms they were either returned to the owner, placed in some child's family, or released. During the first two years the children enjoyed snakes, rats, moles, sand crabs, hamsters, flying squirrels, rabbits, chickens, ducks, fish, turtles, and snails. After even the most timid child in the class held a garter snake, most of the teachers learned to overcome their fears. A child who becomes conscious of the need to feed a rabbit the proper diet may become more interested in eating a balanced diet himself.

Art Enrichment

Some teachers fail to provide the bright, creative, and stimulating classrooms which are necessary if these schools are to become pleasant, productive centers of learning. In many classrooms, the art curriculum was severely limited by the teachers' lack of initiative, their fear of working in new art media, and their over concern with covering the academic subject matter. Teachers' discouragement with the disadvantaged child's lack of success in reading and arithmetic often greatly limits their efforts in the arts. A no nonsense, no fun, no frills, no variety curriculum kills motivation; thus it was decided during the third year of the project to include art enrichment experiences for the experimental children. One of the project's staff members had particular competencies in this area.

An hour-long semimonthly art session was held in each classroom. The two objectives of the program were (1) to provide the students with experiences in different art media, and (2) to create a more pleasant classroom through displays of children's art work.

Once a month, the art session was related to a seasonal motif which could be used as a classroom decoration. While this type of experience may seem to be limiting the pupil's creative ability and freedom to choose his own subject matter, the teacher felt that a moderate amount of structure was helpful to children of this type.

Previous experiences with art, both in the home and at school, had been limited. Most teachers had been using mimeographed pictures which were colored with crayons almost exclusively; therefore, the second session each month was designed to give the children an opportunity to explore different art media. The use of tempera paint and watercolors was combined with craft and construction materials to stimulate the children toward more creative and imaginative efforts. The children's productions were usually sent home. There the displays of pictures and statues made by the children gave evidence that the projects had been given prominence and appreciative attention in many families.

An art exhibit of children's work was accumulated during the year, and an exhibit was displayed at the public library and at a nearby college. Producing a display was not the primary objective of the art program, but recognition of children's abilities in this manner was found to be stimulating. Children who are "behind" academically often get little recognition for their efforts.

Evaluation of this type of activity is difficult. Surely children were interested in improving their own techniques and gained a somewhat greater appreciation for the fine arts.

Some teachers have completed the art sessions begun by the consultant and continued the art program during the subsequent year, thereby indicating that efforts in the area were beneficial. Other teachers, however, took advantage of the consultants' presence to leave the classroom and thus did not take advantage of the opportunity offered them.

After-school Activities

During the spring of the second and third grade years, a garden project was initiated on a half acre of land donated by a local businessman. Each evening immediately after school the children whose parents had given them permission to participate were picked up in staff cars and driven the approximately three miles to the garden site. Each of the fours schools had its afternoon at the garden. The youngsters generally came weekly from late March through July, and occasionally thereafter into October.

After plowing, no tractors or mechanical devices were used to prepare the soil or to cultivate it. The children used hoes and rakes to break up the large clods before planting. Using this method it took several months to plant the entire garden. On the average, approximately twenty children a day participated. The supervision of at least two adults was necessary, particularly on days when senior Girl Scouts were not present.

While half the group raked and hoed, another group discussed the types of seeds that were to be planted or the depth and distance apart of the planting, or engaged in some nature study activity nearby. Every ten or fifteen minutes, jobs were exchanged. Fortunately, during the two years the garden project was conducted, no injuries resulted from overly ambitious hoeing. More than 80 per cent of the experimental group participated in this after-school activity. During the summer, attendance fell off somewhat. At this time children had to learn to get themselves to school at a particular time on a particular day in order to participate, no easy task for young children from families which are not usually "clock oriented."

At school, a large chart was constructed with the names of all the flowers and vegetables which were planted in the garden. Colored pictures were cut from an almanac and pasted under the appropriate names, and the seed of the plant was glued under the picture as well. The planting and harvesting times were recorded on the chart.

On the average, one adult a day assisted the staff and children in planting and cultivating. Often on summer evenings children brought their parents and grandparents to the garden. This activity served to develop an appreciation of nature and useful work, and the importance of planning and taking care of things. The children were proud to take their produce home.

Concerts and Art Exhibits

Thanks to the Fine Arts Society, the Civic Music Association, and a large number of college students, a majority of the project children attended a number of professional concerts. Usually before the concert they listened to recordings of some of the music they would hear. Permission slips were signed by the parents. Children were picked up and returned to their homes. Since almost all of these concerts took place in the evening, the children were treated to a soft drink at intermission time and then taken home. The children enjoyed dressing up, being in a crowd of people in fancy clothes, sitting in soft seats in the half-light, and of course, the soft drinks. The next day the children shared their experience with their entire class at school. They commented on their enjoyment and asked questions about the things which puzzled them, "Why did the singer always close his eyes when he sang, did the lights hurt his eyes?"

The Art Club made their shows available to small groups accompanied by college students or entire classes with their teachers. Sometimes an exhibit was explained by a lecturer, but children were always given plenty of time to look and enjoy. A sorority conducted an art workshop at Whitman for a time. By preparing the students ahead of time to understand some of what they were to see and hear, and by providing them with attractive adolescents to act as guides into the world of culture, we felt that we reduced the psychological distance between the inner city child and Carnegie Hall. Elementary school band and orchestra concerts showed pupils that children could also perform enjoyable music.

More Informal Activities

Some of the after-school and evening enrichment activities didn't require extensive preparation. An ice show, football and baseball games, picnics, and parties, all chaperoned by college students, required less preparation. Best of all one Saturday some Culver-Stockton College fraternities staged a hootenanny. The entertainment was of highest quality, and when the children were encouraged to participate they did so with enthusiasm.

Summer Activities

In addition to the garden project, the Commission sponsored a six weeks reading program during the summers following the first and second grade. This was done because it had been found that most of these children did not ordinarily come into contact with any reading material during the summer, and as a consequence when they returned to school in the fall they had forgotten much that they had learned in reading.

Each year the children who had done most poorly in reading and those whom the teachers and staff had reason to think would have little contact with reading during the vacation were strongly encouraged to come to the school for one hour each morning for six weeks to be given reading instruction in small groups. The program was explained to the parents of this group in a home interview. In addition, children whose parents specifically requested that their child participate were also allowed to come during the first year. During the second semester all children were invited to participate. The vast majority of parents saw the program as worthwhile and saw to it that their children attended.

The first year, two of the family workers and two teachers handled this assignment, but the teachers were found to have better attendance and to be more effective, so during the second year only teachers were used. The teachers liked the program because they had a chance to try out books other than those usually used at school and to try other techniques such as individualized reading if they desired. Having only one reading group at a time with no seat work or disciplinary responsibilities was satisfying, and children and teachers were spared several weeks of review in the fall. Most children could remember to come to school from 9:00 to 10:00 AM or from 11:00 AM to noon, but follow-up home visits were sometimes necessary to insure good attendance.

Summer Day Camp

It had long been the desire of the staff to provide a day camp experience for all of the children involved in the program, but the lack of a site and the staff necessary to make it successful were barriers.

When the question was discussed with the local Girl Scout council, they graciously granted us the use of their camps. Girl Scouts volunteered to act as counselors, and a troop advisor volunteered to serve as co-director of the camp. Six students from a nearby college participated, and one of them agreed to serve as the other co-director.

The day camp was held one week during the month of August. The cost of food, camp supplies, and transportation was borne by the project. The scouts, with their rich camping experience, put their skills to use. They were instrumental in making it possible for us to provide a week of outdoor adventure for a hundred boys and girls who would not otherwise have had such an experience.

The program began with a one-day training session. At this session the scouts were briefed on the problems they might be expected to encounter and how they might best handle them. There was also a discussion of camp regulations and how best to transmit these to the children. A suggested activity agenda was presented by the co-directors, and the scouts were given the opportunity to offer their suggestions and to make changes.

The first day of camp marked the beginning of activities such as nature crafts, outdoor cookery, fire building, and nature hikes. The girls were assisted by the more mature college students.

The project children were given the opportunity to register for the day camp before the dismissal of school in June. All but three of the experimental group children registered and paid the nominal admission fee. This fee, 25c, actually covered only the insurance.

Shortly before the camping period, a group of fathers from the project schools came to camp one Saturday afternoon armed with lawn mowers and sickles. They worked together for a whole afternoon and effectively cleared the camp site, cut the grass, and replaced the flag pole. A mother of one of the project children served as volunteer nurse for the entire four-day camp session.

Teacher Enrichment

Most of the project teachers needed to be exposed to new ideas, new techniques, and most of all to an optimistic viewpoint. Since their practice teaching days most hadn't seen another teacher teach a class, and none had ever been sent by her school to report back on her impressions of another school system or other teaching methods. The project sent teachers to study other programs for disadvantaged children in Milwaukee, Detroit, St. Louis, and Chicago.

The project principals and teachers who visited other systems saw some good teaching being done by persons who themselves were convinced that culturally disadvantaged children had great potential which could be developed. They saw in action a number of curricular modifications advocated by the project staff. The teachers reported back to their faculties and sometimes made individual modifications in their techniques, but no major changes in direction resulted from the visitations. It seemed that once back in the home community the differences between the other system and our own were great enough to convince people that the techniques probably wouldn't work very well here, and besides, teachers don't bring about curriculum modifications that extend beyond their own classroom. Major curriculum modifications come from the top, and in this system directions for changes were not forthcoming.

Some of the teachers, particularly those new to the system, did take advantage of an opportunity presented by their principals to visit classrooms at their grade level in other sections of town while the principal taught the children. Anything which can be done to encourage teachers to communicate with their fellows about methods of reaching and teaching students is worth the effort.

Most teachers lead rather isolated professional lives. The interest of the Commission and the project staff in what teachers were learning from their work with the students was growth-producing for many teachers. This was particularly true of the younger teachers who had not become discouraged and cynical. The staff worked closely with any teacher who evidenced an interest in experimenting with her teaching techniques. If a teacher expressed an interest in Cuisenaire rods, the staff bought some and worked with the teacher in learning to use them. However, the project did not have the money to equip the classroom, a fact which sometimes limited experimentation. Where teachers indicated that they preferred to work alone, the workers confined most of their contacts with them to coffee breaks and after-school conferences on individual children, setting up trips which the teacher wanted to take, and planning parent visits and parent meetings.

Teachers varied greatly in their response to the project. No one asked for a transfer to avoid it, but some told their colleagues, "It only lasts a year, then you can return to whatever you did before—it's not so bad." A number of the inexperienced teachers seemed to appreciate the assistance of the family workers, and when they followed their husbands to other communities, asked for teaching assignments in this type of community. They became convinced that they could respond to the children's needs in an effective manner, and that they had learned something about communicating and educating the disadvantaged and their parents. The staff's effectiveness with teachers varied from almost no influence at all to moderately effective, but major far-reaching modifications in curriculum were not accomplished. The enrichment aspects of the program which took place after school, in the evenings, and during the summer do seem to have had more permanent results, as will be discussed in the last chapter.

Chapter IV

PARENTAL PARTICIPATION
IN EDUCATION

THE THIRD MAJOR objective of the project was to enlist the interest, support, and cooperation of the parents in helping to motivate the child to develop his interests and abilities. Parental involvement was a major objective because the use of whatever intellectual potential exists is determined by the child's environment, and the most potent part of that environment is his family. During the most formative years in life, parents have a tremendous influence on the child's definition of the world and his place in it. It is here that the child learns to trust or fear, to approach or withdraw from new persons or situations; no one else has as strong an influence on a child's motivation, his value system, his view of himself, and his place in the world. The child who spends his preschool years in a home without love or without books will not be as ready for school and will not achieve as easily as one who enters the world of adult-directed learning with a desire for knowledge and a belief that the world is friendly, understandable, and controllable.

While this project could do nothing about the preschool years of these children, the staff hoped to increase the educational value of the child's out-of-school hours. To do this the project staff had to establish meaningful communication with the parents. The initial interview previously discussed in Chapter II was only the first in a continuing series of formal and informal contacts with project parents.

To avoid being regarded as an intruder, the family worker had to be tactful. The initial visit to a family was preceded by a letter suggesting a time for an appointment. Usually each home visit was ostensibly pegged to a specific reason for coming—"We are planning a series of parent meetings this year; what sorts of things would you like to talk or hear about at these meetings?" "What has been Debbie's reaction to our field trips to the hatchery and the orchard?" "Could you go with us when we go to inspect the new factory going up at 30th and Locust?" "Could you spend about ten minutes each evening listening to John read from this book for the next two weeks?" The illustrations which follow will give the reader an idea of the methods employed by the family workers and demonstrate some of the changes which occurred as the result of intensive work with families.

Mrs. Johnson was removed from the rolls of Aid to Dependent Children because she no longer had babies at home and had refused the jobs she had been offered. She felt that she was being discriminated against; but after the family worker heard her out, she accepted reality and with the aid of the worker got enough part-time work as a domestic to support her family. David, her son in the experimental group, had many illnesses which resulted in absences and poor school work. Children can exist on soda, potato chips, and candy bars, but the staff suspected a connection between David's attendance record and his inadequate diet. Mrs. Johnson didn't understand basic nutritional needs, but was willing to work with the family worker to see if this would help David. In the first grade, David's absences were less frequent.

Mrs. Allen, an obese, aggressive mother, stormed into

the kindergarten demanding to know why her daughter was not getting good grades although she was taller and larger than any other child in the room. Mrs. Allen quivered with rage as she struck out verbally against the school administration. Her daughter, Vanessa, was constantly in trouble. Sometimes she just seemed to bump into things, but in addition to being a bull in a china shop she often hit or bit other children. Her mother defended Vanessa's behavior.

The family worker made a number of attempts to see Mrs. Allen, but the appointments were constantly broken without explanation. One day on a street corner, Mrs. Allen and the worker met by accident. They talked at length about Vanessa and the importance of her doing well in school. Following this, for the first time Mrs. Allen was at home for an appointment. She was persuaded to attend several parent meetings and participated in going on a family trip. In time she seemed more understanding of the problems Vanessa faced at school, and also of the teacher's position. The relationship became so cordial that Mrs. Allen sometimes telephoned the worker to talk about Vanessa. The mother's more relaxed interest has helped Vanessa to work to the limits of her capabilities as a student and to develop a more pleasing personality.

Mrs. Babson and her husband were outstanding leaders in the Negro community. They demanded a great deal from Phyllis, their daughter. Phyllis reacted to these high aspirations by crying whenever she lost a game and sobbing at the slightest demands on her in the classroom. Mrs. Babson was extremely friendly with the family worker, but for months was unable to see that the family had anything to do with Phyllis' classroom behavior. Through time there has been a slight but noticeable loosening of the family demands for high achievement, with the result that Phyllis has been able to accomplish more at school.

Mark was the youngest in a family of ten children. Although they had many children, Mr. and Mrs. Coffman had never visited Langley School. The teacher was concerned because Mark was too shy to participate in even the least formal of the kindergarten activities. It was necessary, for example, for the teacher or the family worker to take him by the hand to get him in line for a drink of water or to go to the bathroom. Although he was not resistant, he was passive to the point of being immobile.

The family worker called on the Coffman family. The parents explained that Mark had been seriously hurt by a truck when he was four and that since then he had been very fearful. The family and the worker discussed possible methods of helping Mark venture forth more often. Sometimes Mrs. Coffman promised to come to parent meetings, but she didn't attend one until near the end of the third year. She seemed apprehensive about the reasons for the family worker's visits. Someone at the door from the schools or a social agency spells trouble to many lower status adults, and many such adults see avoidance of trouble with authority as about the best that can be hoped for in this life.

Mark participated in the after-school library trips. Unlike his siblings he began to do well in school; he liked to read. When Mrs. Coffman noted his increased self-confidence, she was able to express her appreciation. She was impressed when Mark, accompanied by an older brother, went on the final family field trip. Mark's behavior has changed noticeably since kindergarten; now the teacher occasionally even has to admonish him for talking.

Charles Dixon was one of the brightest children in the experimental group, but his grades didn't show it. His mother had been divorced and had remarried a man who could not hold a job. She did dressmaking at home. Nevertheless when the stepfather said, "Let's go out," Charles was completely ignored. Neither parent recognized Charles' superior ability, but the mother came to parent meetings if Charles was on the program. Otherwise, the family didn't participate in parent activities.

Charles seems to need to cling to outside adults, but thus far has not had much incentive to work to his capacity. Intensive work with the Dixons over an extended period of time might bring about increased involvement by the parents, but thus far little progress has been made.

Sometimes the project's accomplishments with families were very limited. Sally lived directly across from the school but had a history of absences and tardiness. Mrs. Eric never responded to knocks on the door. The Erics had many marital difficulties; finally Mr. Eric left home and his wife began to "run around." Mrs. Eric always excused Sally's absences by saying that she was ill. She was not convinced that it was necessary for Sally to attend school regularly. Although the mother attended only two parent meetings, she did allow Sally to have a Girl Scout take her to and from the library. This seemed to help Sally's school work. Despite continued cultural deprivation and marital upsets at home, Sally was enabled to succeed fairly well in her classroom work.

Some inaccessible families can be reached only through the success of their children. Mr. and Mrs. Morris seemed almost inaccessible. Mr. Morris was an out-of-town truck driver home only on weekends usually. His wife worked long, hard hours at a factory. It was difficult to make appointments with her, and when she was seen at home she was tense and distraught. Mrs. Morris was a compulsively neat housekeeper who seemingly spent much of her time shouting at the four children. Roger was allowed to run through the neighborhood without supervision—"You can't look out for kids and work too, and I have to work." This was also Mrs. Morris' excuse for not participating in any of the school activities. After four years it seemed that this family would never respond to home contacts.

During the fourth year of the experiment, however, the family worker initiated a preschool Spanish class as a result of a social studies unit on Mexico. Roger, generally an indifferent student who spent most of his time molesting his friends, became intensely interested in learning conversational Spanish. He was the first in his class to be able to carry on a limited conversation. When a puppet show written in Spanish, "The Three Billy Goats Gruff," was used to demonstrate the children's accomplishments in Spanish to the parents, Roger won the leading part, Big Billy Goat Gruff.

Roger came home with the news; and at the next home visit, for the first time, both parents were present. They were full of questions about the foreign language program. Roger, they said, was a different child. He was very enthused about speaking a language that his parents couldn't understand. For the first time their child had done something academic of which they could be proud. The Morrises were encouraged to attend Roger's big moment. They arrived at the parent group meeting with their three other children and were very proud of their son's accomplishments. When all other efforts at getting the family to meetings had failed, this approach brought results.

Some parents were hard to reach because they had previous unhappy experiences with the school. The Gordons, parents of ten, had had many such experiences. Although both were hard-working people, they were not highly thought of in the Negro community because they were quite belligerent. Mrs. Gordon thought little of engaging in fisticuffs with neighbors. Ruth reflected this pugnacious attitude in the classroom as soon as she entered kindergarten. She was uncooperative with the children as well as with the teacher.

The Gordons were particularly upset because five of their children had been placed in classrooms for the mentally handicapped, and they were convinced that anyone who came to see them about Ruth had this in mind. It took almost a year and a half to persuade the parents that we realized that Ruth was of normal intelligence and could succeed in school if she could become less aggressive.

The first parent meeting which the Gordons attended was one in which the parents were fixing up the kindergarten room, sewing dresses, and painting furniture. Mrs. Gordon refused to do any of these things and spent the time talking in a very amiable fashion with the family worker.

The field trip by bus was the first time the Gordon family had ever gone anywhere together. They really enjoyed it. Subsequently Mrs. Gordon was able to say that she was pleased with Ruth's reading at home and her better grades in school. By the fourth year Mrs. Gordon missed very few parent meetings, and many of her misconceptions regarding schoolwork changed. The entire family went on all family trips, and she was the spokesman for a group of Negro parents who wanted to express their feelings about the extra attention their children had received. She put her arm around the worker and said, "We all want to tell you that we want you to know we appreciate your work." This attitude did not carry over into her private life, however, because Mrs. Gordon is still frequently picked up by the police for fighting.

The mental limitations of some of the parents made the family worker's progress quite limited. Mrs. Baxter was always concerned about her health. She said that the doctor thought she might have a "clog on the brain," and that she was on the "urge" of a nervous breakdown. When the family worker brought books to help her daughter Barbara, she told her daughter, "If you don't learn to read, I'll spank you till you can't sit down." It was recognized that Mrs. Baxter's mental limitations, her involvement with her own ailments, her husband's desertion, and her efforts to stretch the aid check involved most of her time. Mrs. Baxter was visited twice a year in an effort to make her feel a part of the experiment, but little was expected of her and little was accomplished.

Mrs. Stanton had even more mental limitations and yet was reached by the project. She couldn't remember which months her children had been born in, couldn't keep track of how much money should be sent to school for school lunches, and could never remember to come to the parent meetings unless a home visit was made on the date of the meeting. Despite an outward appearance of bluster and self-importance, Mr. Stanton was also essentially an illiterate.

The family worker was always greeted warmly by the Stantons, and when they were reminded they came to the meetings. Darlene was very proud of their attendance. Progress in this family as measured by middle class standards was practically nil, but the child valued the home visitor's calls. In this she was joined by many of her classmates. Having a man from the school come to visit your home to talk about you in a positive tone is good for anv child's ego.

Generalizations Concerning the Worker's Relationships With Families

1. If attitudinal changes are to occur, the family worker services must be offered in a nonpunitive fashion. Most of the parents have met a succession of relatively untrained public welfare workers and probation officers and expect home visits to be unpleasant experiences. Like their children, these parents need to feel that they are doing a good job in at least some areas.

2. Parents should be made to feel comfortable enough with the family worker to voice any complaints they have about the school system, and where possible the family worker should attempt to eliminate the parents' cause for dissatisfaction.

3. Family workers should demonstrate to parents how they can help their children with their school work.

4. Family workers should interpret school policies to the parents; when this is not possible, they should take an active role in bringing together the parents and the appropriate school personnel.

5. Family workers can play a useful role as a liaison between teachers and parents. They talk with the parents about the teachers' concerns with the school learning and behavior of the children, and relay to the teachers children's reactions to their school experience. When administrative decisions such as retention were being considered, this was discussed with the families in a tentative way before these decisions were made final.

6. The family workers can sometimes help parents with

specific behavior problems, such as lying, by suggesting possible meanings for these behaviors and some procedures which the parents might try. Follow-up interviews were conducted to review and modify procedures attempted.

7. The family worker cooperated with other agencies working with the family and steered people to proper resources when he was confronted with problems which he was not equipped to handle.

8. The family workers played a useful role in explaining the educational activities of the classroom and after-school programs to the parents.

9. The workers talked with parents about developing their own abilities and expanding their own horizons in the community. As a result of these discussions, several of the parents went back to school part-time.

The family visitation program clearly demonstrated that changes can occur among culturally handicapped families if the school is willing to reach out intensively to families. In doing this, the workers must not only demonstrate that they are willing to listen and attempt to modify their own behaviors in order to help the child, but they must also give the parents something useful to do which will contribute to the educational success of their children. Feedback from parents must be frequent, for they are easily discouraged.

Teacher Visits in the Home

Since the child continues to spend much more time at home than at school, the schools can make little headway with the child if his home continues to foster inappropriate attitudes and habits. Teachers must find ways to overcome parental indifference to education and to help parents support the school's efforts.

Throughout the four years of the project, teachers have been encouraged to make home visits. The primary aim has been to get parents to take a more active interest in their child and his school activities. The visits also provided a means of learning about the family's provision for the child's needs in the following basic areas: food, shelter, and medical care; the emotional warmth of the home; the amount of intellectual stimulation present in the child's physical environment; the time and interest displayed by the parents in the child's intellectual growth; and the value placed on personal achievement.

The home visits have provided a means by which the school personnel can become acquainted with parents. They help to develop a mutually satisfying relationship based upon acceptance and understanding. When parents realize that the school is genuinely interested in the welfare of their child and that meeting with school people can be pleasant and useful, a common bond of interest is developed.

Once the initial teacher contact with the home is made, a more harmonious atmosphere of home-school cooperation prevails. A typical comment made by a parent recipient of a home call is "What did Jimmy do now?" It is rewarding to see this negative attitude change to the positive side when the parents learn the teacher is a considerate, intelligent human being and really does care about Jimmy and his success in school.

To avoid encroaching on the teacher's personal time, the project staff was permitted to substitute in classrooms, thus freeing teachers to make home visits during school hours. A two-hour training workshop examined the conduct of home interviews and what they could be expected to accomplish. The staff role-played a typical home interview.

Teachers were strongly encouraged to participate in this part of the program, and those who did so were pleased with the results. Even so, only six of the twenty-two teachers who participated in the project over the years chose to make home visits.

One teacher became so pleased by the knowledge she gained about the families in her school that she completed visits to the homes of every child in her classroom. This was a particularly good experience for this teacher as she was new in the school system and came from an upper-middle-class family. This teacher stated that:

> This has been a wonderful year for me. I am certain that I have learned as much as the children. It is so different actually getting into the homes than it is reading a case history. I am certain that I knew and understood the children so much better than I have ever understood a group of children before. I felt very close to them.
>
> I had no serious discipline problems this year. There certainly are discipline problems in other rooms and I've had many in other years. Knowing the parents and working together has just meant everything.

It is possible to see change in some children as a result of home visits.

> Joe was an extremely shy, withdrawn boy who had little motivation for school work, lacked the basic foundations of study habits, and had a somewhat fearful attitude of the school. In a home visit to a three room house located on the riverbank, the teacher found parents who had no idea of modern child-rearing practices. The family was fully convinced that if their child did not do well in school that a good sound beating would take care of it and if the first did not take care of it, the second one would. She asked me, "Mrs. Allen, are you tough on my boy?" I said, "No, Mrs. Armstrong, I am not. I never

have had occasion to be." She said, "I can't understand that; he is a holy terror at home." "But," she added, "if he has another easy teacher like you again next year, he won't learn nothing."

After many telephone conversations and personal visits, the family became convinced that Joe was working in class but that he wasn't ready for the third grade work. On her final home visit the teacher wrote, "It was a great surprise and most gratifying to discuss Joe's retention with Mr. and Mrs. Armstrong and to have their permission. When I mentioned to them that he should not be punished for this they said, 'Oh no, we don't feel that way anymore'."

Teacher home visits provide:

1. A development of a common bond of understanding between the home and the school.

2. A promotion of the feelings that the teacher and the school as a whole are sincerely interested in the welfare of the child.

3. Greater insight into the home environment and its effect on the child.

4. A means of letting the parents know first-hand what their child and the teacher are doing at school. It is another means of breaking down the invisible barrier of communication between the home and the school.

Parent Group Meetings

Attendance at PTA in the four project schools was very poor. In some cases the teachers outnumbered the parents who were present. The parents told the family workers that they did not attend PTA meetings because they disliked the formality and the business program. It was evident that a new approach was needed.

Parent meetings have been an integral part of work

with families. They served as an opportunity for the parents to meet on a group basis with other parents having similar problems and children in the same grade. In some of these neighborhoods parents have a strong need for social contact with other families because they do not belong to organized groups other than church groups. The meetings were structured to interpret to the parents what the child was doing at school, to raise the parents' achievement level expectations of their child, and to provide social experiences designed to promote family togetherness.

The parent meetings were held on a bimonthly basis. Every effort was made to reduce social distance and verbal barriers between professionals and parents and to increase the flow of communication. Coffee was served during the meeting rather than after the meeting. Meetings were informal and without officers, dues, or budgets. Typically everyone sat around a table rather than sitting in rows facing a speaker.

Since it was difficult for many of these parents to attend a meeting without a strong feeling of security, the family workers made home visits during which they emphasized the teacher's and project staff's eagerness to get acquainted with the parents and to get the parents' view of their children's education. Baby sitters were furnished, thus eliminating expense as a reason for not attending.

Most of the early parent meetings were built around discussions of five and six-year olds and what they were like—their problems and learnings. Parents wanted to know what the children were learning at school, what materials were being used, what these new methods of teaching reading and arithmetic were all about, and what the report cards meant. Demonstrations by teachers and pupils showed what children were learning at school.

Parents at two of the schools decided to improve the kindergarten classrooms. At Langley, for example, some mothers made curtains while others painted furniture or drew pictures to represent the alphabet. A group of the fathers built a playhouse complete with triple-track aluminum storm windows donated by one of the parents. These parents felt that they had contributed something practical to their children's education. One father said, "I might learn something by sitting down and talking with you people, but I know that Jim will enjoy the playhouse." The informal talk while parent and teacher worked on the playhouse may well have been as important as any child psychology lecture.

Sometimes in the spring, programs centered around summer recreation and what parents could do at home to help their children become better prepared for school in the fall. The first year Ross school finished with a family picnic which drew 130 parents, teachers, and children. Project families had lots of children. This large and enthusiastic get-together paved the way for family field trips in subsequent years.

Some of the parents volunteered to help the family workers plan the parent meetings. Some wanted meetings to address themselves to questions such as: to spank or not to spank, when should I try to see the teacher to talk to her about my child, how should doctor and dental appointments during school hours be handled, how long should I keep him out after he has measles, how can I help him with his reading, or how much should I help with work which is sent home to be finished?

At several meetings a home economist from the Farm Bureau cooked some attractive meals using low cost ingredients, and passed out her recipes.

The public library was used extensively throughout the project. A joint meeting with parents from all four schools was held at the library. The children's librarian presented a program on the art of storytelling and showed the parents how to help their children find books they would enjoy and could read. Since this was a pre-Christmas meeting, it was especially appropriate to encourage parents to buy inexpensive quality children's books.

The family worker at Ross School encouraged one of the parents to suggest that the group take a family trip in the spring. After discussion, the group decided to visit the St. Louis Zoo, 125 miles away. Only members of the child's immediate family were permitted, and no child could come alone or with another family. A charge of a dollar a person was made, and the Youth Commission paid the small additional amount needed for transportation. Parent committees collected the money, called to remind parents the night before the trip, and checked in each family at the bus. At 7:00 AM on a Saturday in May, two buses loaded to capacity began what was for many the longest trip the family had ever taken. At the Zoo each family went its own way, but no one was lost.

In the years which followed, the group took trips to New Salem park and Springfield, Illinois, to see the land of Lincoln. The feeling of camaraderie established by these one-day excursions seemed to permeate the parent meetings throughout the first half of the succeeding year, and the planning for the next trip then carried the group through the last half.

Jack's stepfather had never been to the school, partly because he refused to wear his false teeth or put on dress clothes. When the family worker learned that he took home movies, she asked if he would take movies if the project would buy the film. Several home visits were necessary to persuade him to narrate the film at a parent meeting. The worker previewed the film at his home and helped him think through what he would say, but once the lights went out at the meeting, he lost his fear and did a commendable job. He received many compliments from the group and from his son. He became the "official photographer" for the group, and subsequently never missed a parent meeting.

In all, sixty-three parent meetings were conducted by the staff during the four project years. Through the years there was an increase in the type of meeting which involved children or craft activities which interested parents. During the final year, parent turnouts exceeded 50 per cent in all four schools. Teachers and principals maintained their interest and participation throughout the four years. Considerable persistence was required to build a good parent group. The workers continued the home visits and refused to be discouraged by a few poorly attended meetings. In time, attendance and participation increased, although fully half of the parents still seldom attended. Home visits and newsletters were our principal means of communicating with the nonparticipants.

In general the staff learned that:

1. Informality should be the keynote of any meeting.
2. Parents should be included in planning meetings of interest to them, but the worker needs to be prepared to bring forth a number of ideas.
3. Frequency of meetings is less important than having meetings well planned.
4. Free child care encourages attendance.

5. Lecture presentations are less effective than programs which encourage conversational exchange among parents, teachers, and staff.
6. Gathering parental reactions to the meetings brought about helpful modifications.
7. Having children involved in at least part of the meeting increased attendance.

Newsletters to Parents

In order to maintain a regular contact with parents, especially those who did not participate in parent meetings, a monthly newsletter was established in each of the schools. These informal one-page newsletters served a number of purposes. Each issue summarized in simple language the last parent meeting and told parents what to expect at the next meeting. It told of past and forthcoming field trips and suggested follow-up experiences which might help the child derive greater benefit from the trip—"Ask your child about his trip to the pony farm; see if he knows what ponies eat." "Here are some books which you can get at the library that tell about ponies."

Parents were asked to write briefly on topics such as, "How much rest does a child in the primary grades need," "What one parent thinks of home visits by the teacher," and "How much help should parents give with homework?" It was unnecessary to edit any of the material written by parents other than to correct spelling, and parents were pleased to be requested to contribute their ideas.

When names of those who accompanied the children on field trips, and names of parent-meeting participants were included in the news, the newsletter also bolstered the ego of parents. Occasionally children wrote articles for the newsletter describing classroom activities or field trips;

sometimes they even helped cut the stencils.

Other items sometimes covered in newsletters were: announcement of special TV programs of interest to children, announcement of enrichment events such as library puppet shows, explanation of future special projects such as the garden project or summer day camp, and ideas for helping children with their school work and their homework.

Questionnaires at the bottom of newsletters often gave parents a voice in selecting meeting nights, topics for future parent meetings, and a chance to indicate why they had or had not attended the last parent meeting. The newsletter provided an economical method of consulting with parents and seemed to involve more parents in their children's education.

SUMMARY

1. Home visits served the purpose of gaining rapport between the parents, family worker, teacher, and school. The result was increased parental involvement in the education and personality development of the children.

2. Teachers who visited in the home found the teaching year more productive, but most teachers did not make home visits.

3. With informality the keynote, parent group meetings about meaningful child-related programs became better attended as the project proceeded.

4. Simple newsletters were a valuable tool for maintaining family contact.

Chapter V

UTILIZING COMMUNITY RESOURCES

THE USE OF VOLUNTEERS

Teen-age and adult volunteers contributed thousands of hours of their time to the experimental children. The recruitment, training, and supervision of these volunteers cost about one year of staff time over the four-year period. This was a highly economical use of staff time for two reasons: first, the volunteers contributed several hours for each staff hour spent; secondly, the volunteers' interest demonstrated to the children that many people in addition to their parents and teachers stood ready to help them be successful and happy at school, and that they were not alone in their struggle to master intellectual skills. Volunteers should be a part of any cultural enrichment project.

Since the rewards for this type of work are in the psychological realm, it is necessary to provide satisfaction for the volunteers through supervision. Since preparatory training and supervision take time, in most instances it is not wise to recruit volunteers unless they are willing to contribute a significant block of time to the project. We did not accept the assistance of any college students who were not willing to give at least one afternoon a week to the work for one school year, except for one-time activities such as accompanying children to a concert or a picnic. These children have had too many adults in their lives who professed concern for them but disappeared a few days or weeks later.

The staff carefully briefed the volunteer concerning the child and family he would be working with and the types of activities which were thought appropriate. In turn, if there is to be contact with the parents, the family to be visited should be told about the person who will be coming to see them. All adults should understand that the activities of the volunteers would be in the realm of increasing the child's experiences, not playing Santa Claus. Many of these families have received money or goods from agencies throughout the community. The relationships between the volunteer, family, and child should be clearly outlined to avoid this.

Supervision of the volunteer is also necessary to maintain a regularity of contact. Disappointments on the part of the child if the volunteer does not arrive as planned and subsequent guilt felt by the volunteer have to be alleviated, and should be prevented whenever possible. It is equally important that the volunteer feel that he has a person or group vitally concerned with what he is doing. He should have a chance to report on his activities and to discuss problems as they arise. Since the project personnel were more expert in the behavioral sciences and had known these children for some time, they could frequently help the volunteer understand the child's behavior.

College Students

College students made contributions to the project in a number of ways. A selected group of psychology and education students from Culver-Stockton College came weekly to work with the children during school hours. All students worked at least one afternoon a week for an academic year;

some worked two years.

During the first two years of the program there were no specific routines or organization for the students. This proved unsatisfactory primarily because of the college students' relationship with the teachers. The students reported that they were not sure about the role they should take in the classroom. Many felt they needed to know more about the child's background rather than learning from trial and error. They were unsure how to convey their feelings about such matters to the teacher. They were surprised to learn that principals expected to know of their presence in the building, since they felt rather independent from the school's administrative components. The students felt they were out of place and wanted the teachers to give them more direction in utilizing their time.

To improve the situation, a five-week orientation period conducted by the project director preceded the student's assignment to individual and group work with pupils. The orientation sessions were designed to give the students time to read some of the literature in the field, to become somewhat informed about the skills and present learning tasks of the group of children with whom they would be working, and to provide an exposure to the child's environment, the school, and the neighborhood. Students had access to information regarding the children assigned to them.

Emphasis was also placed on problems involved in working with teachers and principals. The staff stressed the importance of keeping the principal informed of the student's activities in the classroom, and students were urged to discuss their ideas with the teachers before beginning an action program. In their enthusiasm some students came into the classroom with very unrealistic ideas. For example, one student wanted to divide a second grade class into three groups and have each write a play on a Grecian theme. Students were urged to meet their responsibilities in order to avoid hostility or indifference on the part of teachers, and procedures for handling irritations and conflicts between students and teachers were discussed. The orientation sessions enabled the students to become more effective sooner and greatly reduced misunderstandings and conflicts between teachers and students.

Project teachers were free to work or not work with students as they chose; only a small minority preferred not to work with the students. After the first year regular college credit was offered to the students because careful supervision and evaluation was provided by both a college instructor and the project director.

The students' duties have included giving help to individual students and small groups, making posters for classroom displays, relieving the regular teacher of routine duties, attending and conducting meetings of parent groups, providing for special enrichment classes in areas such as foreign language and music appreciation, and editing a school newspaper. They made monthly reports of their activities to the project director. Since many of these teachers had had experience with practice teachers, it was necessary to differentiate the skills and tasks of the college students from those of the usual practice teacher. These students were attempting to understand the problems of disadvantaged youngsters and could learn to work individually or in small groups with them, but we wanted to guard against the teachers' turning their classrooms over to the young college students. After a year or two in the schools in this type of situation, a number of the students returned to these schools for their practice teaching; and several have become teachers in the project schools or in similar schools in other communities.

Students feel that they have made their most valuable contribution by talking and listening to the children. The college students have participated in various classroom activities, making it possible for them to have frequent face-to-face contact with the youngsters. The many short walking field trips with from one to four children have been particularly worthwhile. For example, students took children to a department store to see what kind of things were sold there and ended the trip with a dish of ice cream in the mezzanine restaurant.

On these trips the children developed their speaking and listening vocabularies. They also found that the students saw them as worthwhile persons and that other people were interested in their welfare. In a situation of mutual delight in learning, children discovered that there were many interesting things in the world immediately about them.

A pupil told one of the college students, "You helped us not to be afraid." The student's interpretation of this was, "Perhaps I do not pose the same sort of threat as an authority figure as does a full-time teacher. Perhaps this is why some of them feel free to talk to me." Another student said, "A great thrill occurred when I met the parents of the children I had been working with. I gained a newer understanding of the children the first few moments I observed the parents' personalities. I wished that I could have met the parents before working with the children, for this would have helped me understand them better." Along these same lines, a student wrote, "Just from the short encounter I had with the parents I can see some of the reasons why the children are like they are. I wish I had had more time to talk to them."

The activities of the college students have been planned in a monthly session with their professor at the college, the principal of the school, the family worker, the project director, and the teacher. The teacher and the students see the children under differing circumstances and frequently contribute something new to the understanding of the child. The activities of the students have followed the children from kindergarten through the third grade.

One student was assigned as a student coordinator for cultural events. Under his direction youngsters from the project schools were taken to concerts. He arranged for careful selection of chaperones. Nearly one-half of the entire college student body was involved in this activity. The eager glow of anticipation on the part of the youngsters was matched by the warm response of the college students who were gaining valuable insight into the problems which would one day confront them as future educators or as parents.

As an outgrowth of the tremendous interest shown in the project by the college students, additional follow-up programs have been initiated in our community. A reading and study center is now in progress staffed by students from the college. To demonstrate the development of good physical coordination as well as social graces, dance instruction classes for all third grade children in the four project schools are being provided once weekly. Both activities are experiencing great success, as measured by the children's enthusiasm and growth in skills.

Parents, children, college students, and school personnel have all benefited from the past and the present activities being conducted by these college students. It has been interesting to see how the small group of college students working in the program have made the entire student body aware of the needs of the culturally disadvantaged, motivating them to undertake actions calculated to improve the learning of disadvantaged children. The activities of the students working with our program have served to make a significant contribution to the education of students heading toward careers in teaching, psychology, and related fields.

The fraternities provided a big brother relationship for the children in the project. Some of their group activities included a get-acquainted party, a Halloween party, a Thanksgiving turkey dinner at the fraternity house and a visit to the college campus, and a Christmas shopping tour.

Once the boys had started working with the children in a group, they progressed to the point where they worked individually with the children. Activities in this vein were trips around the community to various points of interest such as the Historical Building, airport, the lock and dam, basketball games, and ferry rides—activities which promoted good times and fun for both the college student and the child.

The disadvantaged children especially enjoyed the contact with the men students. A man who is interested in them is a new experience for many of these children, and a man who is interested in what they are doing at school and in their learning is even more rare and growth-producing. Disadvantaged children need to see that men as well as women are interested in reading, music, art, and children's happiness. Children in mother-centered families and women-taught classes need more contact with non-authoritarian males.

Girl Scouts

Two Senior Girl Scout Troops have volunteered a great deal of their time and talent to the program. After reading about the project in the local newspaper, these girls asked the staff what role they could play in helping disadvantaged youngsters. They first began an after-school story hour in one of the project schools. During the spring they conducted nine story hours with no fewer than thirty children in attendance at each session. Although attendance was good, the girls experienced difficulty in keeping order. After six hours in school young children have had too much sitting and listening; they want to talk and move. Therefore, unless there was an adult present, very often the kids moved around too much and talked during the reading of the story. After the first spring this activity was dropped.

The scouts, however, did not want to stop working when school was out; they continued to be interested in the project. They worked throughout the summer in close association with the children on the garden project mentioned in a previous chapter. The girls gave the young project children someone to look up to, a helpful, understanding and loving older sister.

When a second Girl Scout Troop volunteered, it was decided to let the girls be in charge of a library project. Each scout was assigned to one student, thereby eliminating any crises related to orderliness. Each girl was responsible for meeting her literary protege after school once every two weeks. Together they walked to the library. There the adolescent girl assisted the child in selecting books appropriate to his reading level, read him a story or the beginning of a story at the library, and then took him back home.

Once a month the girls met with the Youth Commission staff to report problems or interesting observations that they had made while helping the children. The children loved the individual attention of the scouts. Children learn best in an atmosphere of mutual delight, and the scouts were often able to provide this combined with the intellectual stimulation of conversation and good books.

During the early stages of the project, the project staff had wanted to provide a day camp experience for all children who were in the program but lack of staff and a camp site made this a difficult hurdle. The Girl Scout Council donated its camp. The girl scouts acted as volunteer counselors and their troop advisor served as director. Six students from Culver-Stockton College assisted. A day camp was held for one week during the summer of the year following the second grade. The details of this camp are spelled out in Chapter III.

During the subsequent school year three Girl Scout troops totaling about forty girls, continued to work with project children. One troop decided to take children on monthly field trips at the end of the school day. Through cooperative planning with school personnel, these trips proved valuable in providing additional background experiences for third grade children.

Many of the scouts found the relationship with the children rewarding. As one scout put it, "I have had several contacts with Georgia's parents. They are really nice people and seem to want the best for their children. They are easy to know and make you feel right at home. They really do appreciate the activities that Georgia and I do together because they do not have too much time to spend with their children since they both work. I might add that I also take Georgia's sister Susan with us. Susan is older but is also in second grade. Both girls are really delightful to work with. I hope they look forward to our outings half as much as I do. This is a very rewarding project. I could just go on and on. I could write a book. The only thing I regret is that I don't have more time to spend with

Georgia and Susan."

Mary was a senior in high school with many musical interests. She was introduced to Carol, a little girl who spent much of her time in school crying over real and imagined hurt feelings. Her mother worked and was unable to devote the time necessary to helping her child. After seeing Carol for approximately eight months, Mary's family left the community. Before leaving, she contacted the family worker for instructions on how to tell Carol she was leaving and was so concerned over the possible effects that she asked if it would be possible to introduce Carol to one of her own friends who would then carry on in the same manner. Meaningful relationships can arise from an originally tenuous relationship initiated by an outside agency.

Adults

In any community there are individuals who have unique interests and talent in fields such as music, drama, radio, mechanics, and dance. Usually such persons are willing to help children who might benefit from the contact. When a child in the experimental project demonstrated talent in art, a private teacher agreed to help her. The child's parents took her to the artist's home every week. Both artist and child were pleased with the results.

A Sunday School class of adults who realize children feel inadequate if they lack sufficient clothing has started a room in one of the schools in which clothing donations are repaired and fitted to children who need them. The women are faithful in offering their services, and the children do not feel demeaned in accepting them.

Mr. and Mrs. Hardy were recruited from another Sunday School class. They did not have children of their own. When they volunteered to help with the enrichment program, a family worker suggested that they work with the Forbes children. Mrs. Forbes is a middle-aged divorcee who lives with her two daughters, Joan and Jane. The father is remarried and lives out of the state. Their cramped second floor apartment is extremely inadequate. Mrs. Forbes' job in a chicken processing plant is hot and unpleasant. Consequently, Mrs. Forbes had what might be called a difficult personality. In fact, everyone in the family was difficult. The family worker prepared the volunteers for this and for the fact that the entire family was obese. The family worker attended the first carefully arranged meeting and helped plan some activities which the Forbes girls would enjoy and benefit from. Subsequent meetings were arranged without the family worker. Although the Hardys encouraged Mrs. Forbes to come along whenever she liked, Mrs. Forbes enjoyed this reprieve from her constant duty with the girls and did not participate.

As the relationship developed on a monthly basis, the girls went on picnics and shopping trips with the Hardys and learned to bowl. Both girls showed the Hardys their torn clothing and how badly they needed shoes, but the family worker stepped in and explained to both parties that gifts should be exchanged only at appropriate times such as Christmas and birthdays. On several occasions Joan's behavior, in order to test the relationship, became erratic enough to necessitate the Hardys' calling the family worker on an emergency basis. She had refused to leave the bowling alley and demanded a large sundae instead of the soft drink which had been offered. She cursed and was rude to Mr. Hardy. The worker helped the Hardys to understand Joan's distrust of men, and this made it possible for them to continue seeing them. After two years of a continuing relationship, the girls have shown definite improvement with the behavior problems, and the Hardys feel a great deal of satisfaction from their efforts.

Mothers as Teaching Aides

At Meredith School the principal designed a program for volunteer mothers. Six mothers participated for six months. Several planning meetings were necessary to help the mothers understand their role. They took groups of approximately eight children on the same reading level and helped them develop better listening habits through storytelling and careful listening to records. The children increased their verbalization by acting out their own stories. Educational games were used extensively. For example, they played "baseball" using spelling words or arithmetic problems to determine hits or outs. If adequate supervision had been provided, this would have offered a good way to give disadvantaged children some additional individualized help. After a time the principal greatly reduced his supervision time, and the parents became discouraged and quit.

COOPERATION WITH COMMUNITY AGENCIES

All communities have agencies which are able to contribute to the well-being of school children. When the project staff became aware of the unmet needs of individual students and groups of students, they brought these needs to the attention of teachers and school administrators, or when appropriate, to cooperating agencies such as Public Health, Mental Health, Family Service, Illinois Public Aid, civic clubs, and the Fine Arts Society. The staff took the position that if a parent did not take the responsibility of getting appropriate medical care for his child, the school and community must attempt to exercise their responsibility.

The County Health Department worked with the project

staff in a number of ways. The Public Health nurses serving each of the schools had often known project families for years. Family workers sometimes came to the nurse with questions about the family, "What kind of cooperation did you have when the school found that Terry needed glasses?" "The Browns seem reluctant to talk with me about Bill's troubles at Langley School. Do you know anything about what happened?"

The health department also provided speakers and materials for parent group meetings. Their dentist showed slides illustrating the importance of brushing teeth. The department provided parent groups with films portraying typical five-year-olds or the fears of children and what parents can do to help the child cope with his fears. The school nurses talked to classes on the prevention and treatment of colds.

The nurses also helped the staff see that children's needs for medical care were met. Where parents did not correct a health problem and did not take advantage of offered assistance, the family worker and the nurse together decided on the appropriate next steps.

George Jackson's problem provides an example of how a family worker, school personnel, and local health services can be effective. George's difficulty with vision was obvious to his teachers. A visual screening test confirmed the teacher's judgment, but a follow-up by the school health nurse to the home failed to get George's parents to take steps toward correcting his difficulty. Additional phone calls made by the family worker and the visiting nurse established the fact that the parents lacked the money to take care of the problem.

The school health nurse contacted a local service club which had funds for providing glasses for needy children.

In this instance even though the financial situation had been resolved, initially it was necessary for the family worker to take the child to and from the doctor's office. However, the child's joy at seeing clearly and his improved school work were enough to convince the parents that it was worthwhile to take the child back for follow-up examinations.

Mental Health

Some agencies in the community are not utilized by families of the socially disadvantaged. Betty Simpson, a very intelligent Negro child, lived with her parents and three siblings in a federal housing project. Upon entering kindergarten she presented a picture of sudden changes in behavior. Sometimes she seemed very happy, but she could become suddenly sullen. Her mother regarded Betty as having an eating problem; she was extremely thin. Additional behavior problems arose after a baby sister was born.

The staff frequently used the Bene-Anthony Family Relations Test to explore a child's attitudes toward himself and other members of his family. On this test statements which are positive or negative in tone and of varying intensities can be addressed to or received from each member of the family. The examiner is able to view the family from the child's point of view to find those persons to whom the child reaches out, those he avoids, and those about whom he is ambivalent.

The family workers sometimes used test results as a starting point for meaningful conferences with parents. In this instance the test indicated that Betty felt rejected by her mother and felt that her older brother received more affection than she. Mrs. Simpson tried to take this into account in living with Betty, but during the subsequent summer Betty poured milk in her father's shoes and set fires in the family apartment and elsewhere in the housing project. Since the problem was beyond the competency of our worker it seemed wise to refer the Simpsons to the Mental Health Clinic, but getting the family to this agency was difficult. A great deal of groundwork had to be laid to encourage the mother. The matter of financial obligations had to be discussed with both the Mental Health Clinic and Mrs. Simpson.

While Betty's problems were not immediately resolved, Mrs. Simpson did broaden her own recreational outlets and eased some of her pressures on Betty. Although Mrs. Simpson was not entirely faithful in keeping her mental health appointments, Betty's behavior became less extreme, and in the second grade Betty became a top student. Before the project ended, the father's financial position improved, and the family moved from the housing project to an individual dwelling. Betty has continued to achieve scholastically and her behavior problems are gradually being reduced.

Illinois Public Aid

The Farley family presented a different type of problem. Jim, the youngest of three children, was set apart in kindergarten by his grimaces and other mannerisms and by his all-round immaturity. During the first home visits, Jim's mother, who displayed the same mannerisms as her son, seemed content to live on her ADC allowance. For some reason, perhaps because it gave her a needed social outlet, Mrs. Farley regularly attended parent meetings and helped with field trips.

The ADC worker and the family worker decided that together they could probably help Mrs. Farley attain a more productive life. They helped her find better living quarters and a sitter for the younger children while she worked for a limited high school certificate. Subsequently she completed a nurse's aid course and secured employment. Her new job enabled her to be almost independent financially. The State now provides only for the children's medical expenses.

Through time and effort, Mrs. Farley has become able to handle other aspects of life in a more mature fashion. The family worker helped her accept the fact that her academic expectations for Jim were unrealistically high. but at the same time helped her find suitable reading materials for him. When Jim's behavior later became very aggressive, the worker referred the mother to the Family Service Agency. Mrs. Farley kept her appointments and ADC paid the small fee.

In contrast to this, the concentration and aid of many community agencies and workers have not helped the Davidsons. Mrs. Davidson lived on ADC with her three children, one born after the father left the family. Again the family worker cooperated closely with the agencies and helped Rhonda, who is in the experimental class, to obtain the glasses she needed in order to do better school work. A Brownie uniform was furnished so that she could enter the Scouting program. Although Mrs. Davidson was a high school graduate, she worked as a dishwasher at a restaurant to supplement her ADC allowance. Although she feared change, she took a nurse's aid training course. She did well and obtained a job in a nursing home where she seemed satisfied. However, after six months she quit, complaining that the staff made statements about the legitimacy of her youngest child. Despite the efforts of the

ADC worker and the family worker, she returned to dishwashing.

In another instance a crippled father was unable to care adequately for his family as a commercial fisherman, but his physical disability and lack of education made it difficult for him to find other employment. After considerable effort, Vocational Rehabilitation got the father enrolled in a watch repair school in another city, and Public Aid agreed to support his family during the training period. Unfortunately, after a few weeks, the father dropped out of school and the family's chance to escape poverty was lost.

SUMMARY

In any community there is a large number of persons who have the skills and personal qualities needed to enrich the experiences of disadvantaged children. Children from large families which have working mothers and often lack a father especially need one-to-one or small group contact with adolescents and adults who will talk with them and listen to them.

The volunteers need to be prepared for their jobs. They should know what the child or children know, and what they are trying to learn. They should not become involved in playing Santa Claus and should not establish a close relationship implying a continuing relationship unless they can commit themselves for a significant period of time.

The recruitment, training, and, most of all, the supervision of volunteers denote an economical use of staff time, but it must be realized that whenever two people share responsibility for working with a child there are bound to be disagreements and misunderstandings which should be handled before they become magnified and cause a break in the relationship between the volunteer and teacher or volunteer and child.

Teachers, the principal, the nurse, social worker, and psychologist should get together to make a plan to meet the child's educational needs. Community agencies and the schools can become more effective if they avoid duplication in collecting information for diagnosis and jointly plan their assistance to a family.

Chapter VI

RESEARCH FINDINGS

In THIS CHAPTER the experimental and control groups will be compared, and various subgroupings of children within the two groups will be examined. There are four major types of research outcomes: changes in measured intelligence, differences between groups in achievement areas, such as reading and work study skills, attendance data, and differences in children's feelings about themselves as measured by the self-concept instrument.

Those Who Left

During the four years from the beginning of kindergarten to the end of the third grade, 35 per cent of the children in the study had moved from the community or had enrolled in parochial schools. These students were not included in any of the pre-post test comparisons. Table IV would seem to indicate that somewhat more of the children of the experimental group who scored initially low on the WISC and who were judged to come from families which were considerably handicapping remained throughout the study. The children who left project schools had higher IQs than those who remained in both the experimental and control groups. Thus the children who were lost to the study tended on the average to be a "cut above" the families who remained in the project. These comparisons may be found in Table IV.

TABLE IV
THOSE LOST FROM THE STUDY
AS COMPARED WITH THOSE REMAINING

Group	Mean WISC	Degree of Cultural Handicap (Present)		
		Considerable	Moderate	Little or None
Lost Experimental	95.0	34	29	37
Remaining Experimental	91.7	51	28	21
Lost Control	95.4	48	24	29
Remaining Control	94.5	40	29	31

Intellectual Tests

Table V summarizes the WISC and Peabody test results. The control group had higher initial scores on both tests. Their pre-test superiority on the Peabody Picture Vocabulary Test was significant at the 1 per cent level of confidence, t=3.06; their higher WISC scores were not statistically significant.

On the post-test the experimental group improved their scores on both sections of the WISC and on the Peabody. The control group improved on the performance section of the WISC and got lower Peabody scores. When the results were subjected to a univariate analysis of covariance which statistically corrects for the dissimilarity on the pre-test, it was found that the experimental group's gains on the verbal section of the WISC and on the WISC total score were significant at the 5 per cent level of confidence. The greater gain scores of the experimental group on the performance section and the Peabody were not statistically significant. The gain scores on the WISC total and the verbal subtest were on the order of three IQ points. Despite the modest gains of the experimental group, stability through the four years was more common than radical change. The pre- to post-test correlations for the tests were as follows: WISC verbal .74, performance .73, total .80, and Peabody .71.

A group intelligence test, The California Test of Mental Maturity, was administered by the classroom teachers at the end of the second grade. The scores on this test averaged more than ten points higher than the individual tests given by the psychometrist. The experimental group's higher score on this test was not statistically significant.

TABLE V
ANALYSIS OF COVARIANCE, SUMMARY TABLE

Test	Mean Group IQ Exp.	Control	Source of Variation	df	Adj. Sum Squares	Mean Squares	F Ratio	Level of Significance
	90.1	92.5	Treatment	1	513.4	513.4	5.60	
	93.3	92.5	Individuals	293	26443.9	90.3		
WISC Verbal								
Pre	90.1	92.5	Treatment	1	513.4	513.4	5.69	5%
Post	93.3	92.5	Individuals	293	26443.9	90.3		
WISC Performance								
Pre	94.7	98.1	Treatment	1	140.9	140.9	1.72	N.S.
Post	99.5	100.2	Individuals	293	24065.3	82.1		
WISC Total								
Pre	91.6	95.9	Treatment	1	399.9	399.9	6.02	5%
Post	94.7	95.9	Individuals	293	19458.7	66.4		
Peabody								
	91.7	97.8	Treatment	1	17.0	17.0	.17	N.S.
	92.8	95.8	Individuals	297	29453.7	99.2		

Comparison of Scores by Degree of Cultural Disadvantage

When the WISC scores of the children were grouped on the basis of the child's degree of cultural handicap as measured by the initial home interviews, differences between adjacent degrees of handicap were significant at at least the 5 per cent level in every instance for each group. For example, those youngsters in the experimental group who were judged to have been considerably disadvantaged by their family had significantly lower scores on the initial WISC than did those who were only moderately handicapped (at the 5 per cent level of confidence); see Table VI.

The experiment was especially beamed at the more disadvantaged youngsters, but perhaps it was the socially mobile families with middle class orientations who took advantage of the project. Table VI breaks down the total scores by the degree of cultural handicap. The results would seem to indicate that the most handicapped and the least handicapped improved their scores more than the group from moderately handicapping families. The difference was statistically significant only for the most handicapped children in the experimental group.

TABLE VI
SCORES ON THE WESCHLER
BY DEGREE OF CULTURAL HANDICAP

Degree of Handicap	Mean Pre-test	Mean Post-test	Mean Change	Number of Pupils
Experimental group				
Considerable	86.9	92.2	5.3°	68
Moderate	92.2	94.0	1.8	38
Little or none	102.8	107.8	5.0	28
Control group				
Considerable	88.1	90.1	2.0	63
Moderate	92.4	93.3	.9	46
Little or none	104.9	104.7	−.2	49

°Pre-post difference significant at the 5% level of confidence

How might this differential in improvement be accounted for? The staff made a special effort to see to it that the most handicapped children received the benefits of working with the college students, the scouts and other volunteers. They made every effort to have the most handicapped children attend the summer reading program and other enrichment activities, and worked intensively with the parents of these children. These activities may account for the improvement of the most disadvantaged.

The children of the more adequate families also improved, perhaps because their parents made a special effort to see that their children participated as fully as possible.

Families Having Children in Both Groups

It was thought that families having children in both the experimental and control groups could furnish clues relative to the impact of the enrichment aspects of the program. Since these children generally had the same teachers and the same parents, group differences might logically be attributed to the effects of field trips, summer programs, the efforts of volunteers, and work with project teachers. Generally the test results indicate that on the WISC and Peabody tests the average scores of control group children went down through time while the experimental group's scores improved.

TABLE VII
INTELLIGENCE SCORES OF PUPILS
HAVING SIBLINGS IN THE OTHER GROUP

Group	Test	Mean Pre-test	Mean Post-test	Mean Change	Number of Pupils
Experimental	WISC Verbal	88.7	92.5	3.8	20
Control	WISC Verbal	93.9	91.1	−2.8	22
Experimental	Peabody	90.7	92.6	1.9	20
Control	Peabody	94.2	91.2	−1.3	22

Achievement Measures

The original plan was to use the Iowa Test of Basic Skills to measure achievement at the end of the third grade. The work study skills and the reading sections were given to the control group by their classroom teachers at the end of the third grade. Unfortunately at this point the Iowa Tests were revised and the school system switched to a new test. After some effort enough copies of the earlier form were secured to enable the project staff to give the same form to the experimental group at the appropriate time. Differences between staff-administered and teacher-administered intelligence tests lead us to think that the project staff may have administered this test more strictly than did the teachers during the previous year.

The experimental group was insignificantly ahead on the work study skills and the control group on reading skills. On the average, both groups were reading at grade level at the time the Iowa Tests were given. This is a significant achievement in a group in which only nine of 748 parents interviewed were college graduates and less than 6 per cent reported any educational experience after secondary school. Sixty-five per cent of the parents in the control group and 77 per cent of the parents of the experimental group did not complete high school.

TABLE VIII
IOWA ACHIEVEMENT TESTS—THIRD GRADE

Test	Mean Grade Level		Standard Dev.		Pupil N		Critical Ratio	Significance Level
	X	C	X	C	X	C		
Work study skills	3.4	3.3	.53	.59	85	110	1.22	N.S.
Reading	3.8	3.9	.87	1.26	100	108	.99	N.S.

School Attendance

Each year both groups' attendance improved relative to the previous year's attendance. The absence rate in the third grade was less than 6 per cent, while in kindergarten the rate was 11 per cent. There were no significant differences between the experimental and control groups in any year or over the four-year span. Perhaps this amount of reduction in absence rate could be expected as children get older. The school system's records did not enable us to determine if this reduction was greater than normal.

When the children having siblings in the group were compared, the experimental pupils had been present 93.7 per cent of the time, the control group 92.9 per cent, a difference too small to be significant.

TABLE IX
ATTENDANCE

Group	NC	NX	Mean %		Standard Deviation		Critical Ratio	Level of Significance
			X	C	X	C		
Grade								
Kdg.	163	202	89.8	88.2	10.1	10.0	1.51	NS
1st	191	154	91.4	92.5	10.4	9.5	.99	NS
2nd	173	142	92.9	93.8	6.7	7.7	1.19	NS
3rd	163	151	94.4	94.2	7.6	4.8	.24	NS
Total	192	213	92.0	92.2	6.2	5.0	.41	NS

Self Concept

Lower status children frequently become discouraged in school and decide that they cannot learn. This attitude is thought to play a significant role in their passivity in class, in their difficulty in doing well on tests, and ultimately in their decision to withdraw from school. Therefore, the project made a long-term conscious effort to give the children the idea that they could learn and that they were learning. Unfortunately some of the classroom teachers did not catch this spirit.

To measure children's conceptions of themselves as learners, we administered the "Self Concept As A Learner" test developed by Walter Waetjen as modified by Liddle for use with younger children. Waetjen's subtests—motivation, task orientation, problem solving, and class membership—did not hold up as factors, but since the items seemed meaningful to the pupils, and since the test-retest reliability was satisfactory, we decided to use the test. The test, which may be seen in the Appendix, contains items such as: "I find it hard to remember things"; "I get scared when I'm called on in class"; and "When school work is hard, I usually give up."

When nineteen students were given the test twice at an interval of three weeks, they scored 79.5 per cent of the items in the same fashion. On all administrations of the test, the children had the test before them, but the items were also read aloud by the examiner.

We asked teachers to list the five experimental group children whom they thought would score the highest, and the five who would score the lowest on the self concept instrument. The twenty-eight children nominated as having high self concepts had average scores of 29.7 while the twenty-one low self concept children averaged 24.1 with standard deviations of about 3.5. The two distributions of scores scarcely overlapped. Only two children thought by teachers to have high self concepts had scores below the average of those nominated as having low self concepts; and conversely only two nominated as having low self concepts had scores above the mean of the high group. Thus, teachers seem to be able to predict children's self pictures reasonably accurately. This in turn gave us greater faith that the students were filling out the instrument honestly.

As is shown in Table X, the experimental group had significantly higher scores on the self concept instrument than did the control group, although the difference is a rather small one.

TABLE X
SELF CONCEPT OF EXPERIMENTAL
AND CONTROL GROUP CHILDREN

Group	Mean Score	Standard Deviation	N	Critical Ratio	Significance
Experimental	27.6	4.52	138		
				2.27	5%
Control	26.4	4.57	152		

Teachers As Prophets

In the kindergarten and first grade, we asked teachers to nominate those children whom they could predict would face serious academic difficulty in grade school and who would probably drop out of secondary school. We also asked them to predict which youngsters would do well academically in school. Children nominated by both their kindergarten and first grade teacher in a negative manner were given a score of zero, those so nominated by one teacher a score of one; those nominated by one teacher on the positive side were given scores of three; and those receiving a positive mention by both teachers a score of four. As we move from two negative nominations toward two positive nominations, the percentage of children judged by the interviewers as being severely disadvantaged falls from 76 per cent of the group with two negative mentions to 68 per cent to 25 per cent to 13 percent. The percentage of children with two negative nominations who were judged by interviews as coming from homes which were average or above, that is, not intellectually handicapping in these four categories, was as follows: 3 per cent, 6 per cent, 42 per cent, and 66 per cent. In other words, the children nominated by teachers as likely to have considerable academic difficulty in school came from families rated by the family workers as culturally handicapping, and rarely did they come from families that were thought to be average or above average in this respect. On the other hand, those children who were thought by kindergarten and first grade teachers as likely to do relatively well in school were much more likely to come from average and above average families as rated by the family workers.

The average IQs of children given two negative mentions by teachers was approximately 77; of those given one negative mention, 81. Of those given one positive mention, average IQ was 100, and of those given two positive mentions, 110. Thus, it would seem that teachers' judgments and the judgments of home visitors correlate highly, and their judgments correlate with the results of intellectual measures administered in the kindergarten.

When we looked at changes in the intellectual level of children nominated by teachers, we found that the experimental group children improved their intelligence test scores in each of the four categories, while the control group remained essentially unchanged. On the average, children nominated by the teachers showed a gain approximately four IQ points in excess of that of the control group children in similar categories.

TABLE XI
WISC SCORES OF PUPILS NOMINATED BY TEACHERS

Group	Nominations	Mean WISC Pre	Post	Change
Control	2 negative	80.0	82.3	2.3
Experimental	2 negative	73.9	78.9	5.0
Control	1 negative	77.9	81.8	3.9
Experimental	1 negative	83.7	88.4	4.7
Control	1 positive	103.6	103.3	−.3
Experimental	1 positive	97.3	100.7	3.4
Control	2 positive	112.3	108.0	−4.3
Experimental	2 positive	108.2	112.4	4.2

It was encouraging to note that the project staff indicated that they had had considerable contact with ten of the fourteen children given two negative mentions, a percentage considerably in excess of the percentage for the experimental population as a whole. The project staff did not concentrate their efforts on working with the cream of the crop in the deprived neighborhoods.

Contact with Children and Families

The terms little, moderate, or considerable in referring to the project's meaningful contact with a child or his family are relative terms. There was some interaction with every child who remained in the project for more than a few weeks, and almost all the parents were interviewed on a number of occasions. Thus even the category "little contact" would include many families whose communication with school personnel was much more frequent than is common in this type of neighborhood.

When we examine Tables XII and XIII we see that generally the project had somewhat more contact with the children and families who were most disadvantaged and least contact with the nondisadvantaged children and families. The exception to this pattern is that the project staff had considerable contact with about a third of the families which were judged not to be culturally handicapping. Much of this contact was initiated by the parents, ambitious for their children, while more of the contact with disadvantaged families was initiated by the project staff in an effort to establish communication with parents.

TABLE XII
AMOUNT OF MEANINGFUL CONTACT
WITH THE PUPIL AS RELATED TO HIS
DEGREE OF CULTURAL DISADVANTAGE (PERCENTAGE)

| Degree of Disadvantaged | Child's Contact with Project | | |
	Little	Moderate	Considerable
Considerable	46	29	26
Moderate	48	30	22
Little or none	64	20	16
Total	51	27	22

TABLE XIII
AMOUNT OF MEANINGFUL CONTACT
WITH THE CHILD'S FAMILY AS RELATED TO THE
CHILD'S DEGREE OF CULTURAL DISADVANTAGE
(PERCENTAGE)

| Degree of Disadvantaged | Family's Contact with Project | | |
	Little	Moderate	Considerable
Considerable	52	28	20
Moderate	55	33	12
Little or none	60	7	33
Total	55	24	21

Parental Education and Pupil Achievement

We have previously demonstrated that children's IQs are correlated with the degree of cultural disadvantage as measured by parent interviews. Similarly, as is shown in Table XIV, parental education is also related to children's initial IQs. While only the mother's education is reported in the Table, the results for fathers were quite similar.

The achievement tests administered by the staff in the third grade yielded similar results.

TABLE XIV
CHILDREN'S IQ AND ACHIEVEMENT IN RELATION TO MOTHER'S
EDUCATION—X GROUP

Mother's Education	*Mean WISC Verbal*	*N*	*Mean Iowa Work Studies Grade Place*	*N*
Unknown	89.1	16	2.9	4
Grade school	88.3	45	2.8	17
Dropout 7-10th	88.3	57	3.0	28
Dropout 11-12th	94.8	42	3.1	15
High school grad. or more	103.0	41	3.3	17

SUMMARY

In this study the experimental and control group children grew up in the same neighborhoods and schools and almost always had the same teachers. Whatever differences as groups occurred in the outcome measures may reasonably be attributed to the experimental program—to the enrichment program and the efforts to involve the parents.

The subjective judgment of the project staff and the school personnel who watched the project led us to expect significant differences on most outcome measures, although the consensus was that the control group by chance started a "cut above" the experimental group.

The outcome measures would seem to indicate that the experimental group began the experiment somewhat more disadvantaged than the control group in that their parents were less well educated, their IQ scores were lower, and their reading readiness test results were a little poorer. Despite these initial handicaps, at the end of the project the experimental group had caught up to the control group on intellectual and achievement measures and had somewhat more positive pictures of themselves as learners and as classroom citizens. They had significantly improved their scores on intellectual measures.

This improvement in the experimental group was evident in the children of the most disadvantaged; and in fact, this group improved more on the average than those who were only moderately disadvantaged. The project did seem to reach and help the primary target group, but even at the end of the project one cannot fail to note that most of the children were still disadvantaged. They were and still are being damaged by some aspects of their school and out-of-school environments, and will need further assistance if they are to contribute their proportionate share to the advancement of mankind.

Chapter VII

IMPACT ON THE SCHOOL SYSTEM
AND THE COMMUNITY

Bʏ ᴇxᴀᴍɪɴɪɴɢ aspects of this project which will live on in the community and those which have died or will die, one can evaluate the impact of the project upon the school system and the community. This type of analysis also makes it possible to learn what conditions make for the life or death of an idea in a school system or in a community.

To have maximum impact, an educational experiment should be closely observed by those responsible for making educational policy decisions. The Board of Education and the central administration should be looking over the shoulder of the teachers and project staff to sort out from what is tried those aspects of the program which can, with or without modification, become a part of the ongoing program of the schools.

Almost any program reaching outside a single classroom costs money, and when money is involved the power structure must also be involved. By this criterion the project began badly but through the years grew steadily to a moderately satisfactory position. In the early years of the project there was no face to face contact with the Board and little communication with it. Liaison between the project staff and the schools was handled by a then new assistant superintendent. In time three factors gave the project the ear of the Board and the community: first, through interlocking memberships, the Board of Education became better acquainted with the activities of the Quincy Youth Development Commission; secondly, the assistant superintendent during the fourth year of the project became the superintendent; and lastly, favorable publicity about the project gave it a community-wide audience. As several hundred people in the community made contributions to the program, word of mouth support for enrichment activities and parent-school cooperation increased.

The Commission

The Quincy Youth Development Commission was formed ten years before the beginning of this project to advise the University of Chicago research staff. It helped the community become aware of the research staff's activities, but had no control over staffing or budget. During the second year of this project, the Commission changed from a large rotating group of forty to a nine person self-perpetuating board with financial responsibility for this project. The Commission met bimonthly to review the activities of the staff and to offer suggestions particularly in the area of utilizing community resources and making the community aware of the project and its implications, without conveying the idea that lower status families were being manipulated.

Evaluation of the Project by Principals

Several months after the conclusion of the project, the Superintendent asked each of the principals involved for their evaluation of the impact of the curriculum enrichment program on their school. One of the principals submitted the following report:

I can see some very definite differences in the students of this program in comparison with the other students of our school. These children seem to be a happier group with confidence and enthusiasm. They show this enthusiasm in class response and any activity they enter into. As a group they are more friendly to the faculty and staff. Some individual students I have noted developed a much greater self concept than they likely would have, had they not been in this program.

The parents in general seemed to develop a more positive attitude toward the school and faculty. In parent meetings held this year concerning the school and home working together on homework assignments, the project parents have by far had the best representation at the meetings.

In my opinion the school staff has taken a greater interest in the problems confronting the deprived child and have been willing to exert extra effort to provide for his needs rather than teach the curriculum alone.

In the school community, I feel sure there is an improved feeling of belongingness, especially on the part of the poorer and deprived families. Also, I feel there is a tolerance and better understanding of the poorer people by the middle class or more economically stable population. This is exhibited through the willingness to work together for the benefit of all the children and school without feelings of prejudice and discrimination.

As far as the school system in general, I believe there is a growing awareness of the need to recognize that disadvantaged or educationally deprived children can be helped to develop into successful students and that they can make a worthwhile contribution to society.

As teachers became directly involved with the Program they were given special help through visits to other school systems, where they were able to observe different methods and materials. They were introduced to new ideas through in-service workshops and discussions, both in our own community and in others. They were encouraged to explore new ideas, develop new techniques, and to utilize more fully, not only new materials, but old materials as well.

All of these things brought a new spirit into the planning of the entire staff. There has seemed to be a new interest, a new alertness, a rather competitive spirit in working together. There has been a greater willingness to try different methods in the classroom and a broadening of interest both as individuals and as a group.

The willingness to share and pool ideas with others has shown a marked increase as a result of the special attention given to it during the years the program was in operation.

The parent contacts and parent meetings seem to have borne fruit; however, this is difficult to measure. We seem to notice an improvement in our relationships with parents in a one-to-one situation. Also, there seems to be an improved attitude in answering our requests for assistance on field trips and allied activities.

As we have conducted a series of "open house" programs, room by room, this year we have had an almost 50 per cent average attendance. This is an outstanding record for this school. There has also been fine interest generated in learning about school problems, learning problems of pupils, and classroom activities as shown at each grade level. How much of this interest is a result of previous contacts through the Enrichment Program is difficult to measure.

The school community has reacted favorably, and in a continuing way, to the Enrichment Program. The P.T.A. group has developed programs around child growth and leadership activities. The organization has also become interested in scouting and now sponsors and helps finance it.

Another principal indicated other examples of the continuing impact of the program on his school and school community. He stated that teachers were making increased use of community resource people as a result of their experience in the project. The pre-kindergarten program had been found to be an excellent introduction to school and had been continued. The PTA had shown an increasing interest in the basic problems of the school through their own programs and through their cooperation with the school in various activities which the staff had promoted.

> The social learnings which were gained through field trips, symphony concerts, and dramatic presentations, as well as other areas of the program, have also carried over. The conduct of the children involved in the classroom, the school lunchroom, and on the playground is superior to what could otherwise be expected of them. We feel that this development of self control stems from the special attention given to it through the enrichment program. Even though this particular group of children seem to have more learning problems than other groups we have had, they seem to be doing better academically than we had expected them to do.

A third principal listed similar benefits from better home-school relationships and from enrichment experiences which acquainted the children with the community and enriched their speaking and writing vocabularies. He said that he believed that every activity engaged in by these children was wholesome and educationally sound. He was disappointed that certain of the parents seemed unaffected by the program. He had hoped that they would participate more enthusiastically.

The fourth principal came to his job during the fourth year of the project. While he also voiced similar positive feelings about the project, he did have some negative things to say. For example, he said:

> The children are bored with school this year; there is no glamour or excitement. They sit back and wait for

everything to be done for them. . . . The pupils started to take the added advantages for granted and had to be reminded at times that although they were a favored lot, many did not show good school citizenship to a degree commensurate with their privileges. . . . However, for the most part, I feel that the curriculum enrichment program has done a great deal to make for a better understanding between school and the community. I also feel that the effects of this program will be reflected in the future progress of the students as well as in the future teaching of the teachers who have been involved in this program.

The negatively toned comments by this principal are similar to some of the statements which have been made about Operation Head Start in some of our major cities. Children who have had a good educational experience with sympathetic teachers, a wide variety of materials, and an opportunity to make the entire community their classroom sometimes object to being returned to the sameness and dullness of a classroom in which the teacher feels that she is expected to educate a relatively large number of culturally disadvantaged children without significant help from home-school visitors, parents, or community resources.

Evaluation of the Project by Teachers

At about this time an assistant superintendent interviewed each of the fourth grade teachers who were teaching former experimental group children. One of the teachers expressed ideas which parallel those of the last principal. She said,

I was afraid that when the project was over, students would be let down because they wouldn't be taking part in all sorts of activities. This has turned out to be the case. The glamour is gone. They are not enthusiastic.

They are not responsible. They wait for a leader or for the teacher to take the initiative.

The other three teachers interviewed by an assistant superintendent seem to have been able to build on the strengths of the project children and have thus continued the enthusiasm. One said:

> This is the best year I have ever had. The students are more aware of each other. They sense each other's problems. They know each other's strengths and weaknesses. They concentrate on the strengths. They help each other. There is much more *esprit de corps* this year. They cooperate both in school work and at play. They have a much better background of experience. It is difficult to mention anything that they don't know something about. . . . The parents have been much more cooperative. They have taken more interest in the pupils. We won the room prize at PTA this month.

Another teacher mentioned the increased responsiveness of her children.

> They will listen more attentively than other groups even to subject matter which might be dull, for example, myths. They are more inclined to talk about things which they have seen. They use the Bookmobile, and are competing to see who can bring the most interesting books from home. This is unusual.

Still another said,

> They really enjoyed the trips and other special experiences they were given. This has been helpful in understanding things we have studied. . . . This group has wider interests. I don't have to promote going to the library. They like to go, and go on their own. . . . I think there was great benefit to the project. It just wasn't enough. The students are likely to slip back into disinterest. The parents won't continue the trips without assistance.

The project staff believes that even without assistance the children will continue to be somewhat better prepared to succeed at school, and they will probably be somewhat more enthusiastic than other groups have been, at least for a time. But, without the assistance of some type of home-school liaison person, and without someone to recruit, train, and supervise volunteers, the students, parents, and teachers are almost sure to lose their enthusiasm and return to the status quo.

Perhaps because other experimental programs in this community have usually died once the outside financial assistance was withdrawn, most of the teachers did not expect the program to have a long-term impact. They regarded it as their duty to work a little harder during the experimental year and to go along with the experimental aspects of the program, but they doubted that they would receive long-term assistance with field trips, volunteers, and parent visitation; thus many did not become too involved. Since the administrative committee and the Board of Education never made a study of what it would cost to continue or expand more aspects of the program through local funding, their skepticism was largely justified. Now it seems that Federal funding, such as that of Head Start, has made it possible for many significant aspects of the program to be continued.

The Parents

The gradual increasing attendance at parent meetings indicated greater parental involvement with the school. In three of the four project schools, the project rooms won the attendance prize at the first fall meeting, a prize usually won by kindergarten or first grade classes. Project parents are on the Board of every one of the PTAs, and at Ross they comprise about 50 per cent of the Board. The project has led more of the parents to view the school as a worthwhile institution composed of people of good will who are interested in their children's education. Whether or not the parents will continue to hold this view depends upon the meaningfulness of subsequent contacts with the school at PTA meetings and in other situations. It would have been worthwhile to have principals continue to visit the homes of children new to their schools. Some principals did this for a time without pay or encouragement, but in time this died out. The principals' learnings from their visits did not die out, however.

In a number of ways families have demonstrated that they thought the project worthwhile. Attendance at all types of activities increased through the years. In the school with a 50 per cent Negro population, the family picnics and the three out-of-town family field trips have promoted a feeling of comradeship between the races. The movement of a number of families to more adequate housing has been facilitated by the casework efforts of the staff, but three families who moved to middle-class neighborhoods continued to transport their children to project schools until the project ended.

Impact Upon the Community

The June kindergarten had been continued by the school system in all of the project schools. In the summer of 1965, this effort was replaced by a greatly expanded effort, Project Head Start. The experimental project served as a guide for the Head Start program in Quincy. The program is now operating on a year-round basis under the direction of one of the family workers, Mrs. Sacadat. Since community agencies and the school had learned to work together during the experimental project, they experienced little difficulty in jointly planning and carrying out the new program.

During the summer of 1965, a small civic club anxious to help disadvantaged children after the project closed opened a reading and study center. They raised a limited amount of money, bought the necessary reading materials, recruited some volunteer tutors, and began to work with children. Attendance was good, but the volunteers needed professional assistance, and this proved too expensive. When it looked as though the reading and study center would have to close, a group of college students with the assistance of a teacher from a project school took over its operation.

At least for the present, the college students are continuing almost all of their activities in the schools including the trips to cultural events. This is being coordinated at the request of the superintendent by the Head Start coordinator. The Fine Arts Society provides the tickets, the schools send home notices for parent signatures, and the college students, under the direction of a student liaison person, provide the transportation and supervision of the children. Thus far, not a concert has been missed.

Under the supervision of a college instructor, a number of college students still work with disadvantaged children half a day a week. This will probably continue unless there are major breakdowns in communication between students and classroom teachers.

The dance program begun by three college students during the project years now meets Saturdays at the YWCA. Fourteen students are teaching more than a hundred children. In these classes experimental children and others continue to appreciate music and dance.

The children's librarians also report that continuous exposure to the library from kindergarten through the third grade, the encouragement of the school staff, and the family worker's stress to parents on the importance of reading have continued to bring more of the project children to the library. They also report that the library is being used by larger numbers of children from the project schools who were not involved in the project.

The Girl Scout groups have asked if they might participate in follow-up work with the youngsters they had worked with in the past. For the present they are continuing to take the children on outings; they want to continue. Long-range continuation and expansion of this type of volunteer effort will not take place unless someone is paid to coordinate these efforts and to handle the organizational and interpersonal problems which inevitably arise.

SUMMARY

Many of the results of the experiment do not lend themselves to statistical measurement. For example, the children became less fearful of dealing with people who formerly represented a threatening authority; they feel "at home throughout the city, not just in their neighborhood." They came to have an appreciation of a wider variety of stimuli and learned something of other subcultures in the community. A class trip to a restaurant gave children a glimpse of another environment in a pleasurable fashion. Their exemplary behavior at ice shows and concerts indicated that they were absorbing the social context as well as the sensory messages of the artistic media. Comments at an art show sometimes indicated new appreciations, "Boy, that was a plenty funny picture of a girl holding a cat. I liked it."

The statistical findings indicated that these children are not falling further and further behind as they grow older.

As a group, they are operating nearly at grade level. What differences did exist between experimental and control groups favored the experimental children even though they often had the same parents and same teachers as did the control group.

The project awakened considerable latent interest on the part of at least a large proportion of lower status parents. It evoked significant expenditures of energy in behalf of the target children and families. Adolescents, college students, and adults in all parts of the city entered into significant communication with disadvantaged children and families. The project encouraged interagency cooperation and planning. It made a good beginning in reducing interracial and interclass tensions. It broadened the concept of community for all its participants.

Despite the good beginning achieved, every individual and every community has a tendency to return to the narrow and self-centered way. It therefore needs planners and communications experts similar to the project's family workers. It needs persons who can see the broad picture and have the time and energy to bring people together to face the problem of making childhood a more significant experience, and parenthood and teaching more significant adult roles. Those who participated felt that they had found at least partial solutions. They leave the experience satisfied that the effort has been worthwhile, and that increased intelligent educational planning and evaluation will result in a more significant education for children from disadvantaged families.

APPENDIX

NOTE TO PARENTS FOR GARDEN

We think that children can learn a lot and have fun working in a classroom garden with other first graders from their school. We hope to have those children who are interested, plant a garden, take care of it, and watch it grow and then share in the harvest. Land for the garden for the first grade children has been donated and is located about one half mile southwest of 8th Street. The children will work in the garden one afternoon each week. They will be transported to the garden at the close of the school day and returned to the school by no later than 5 o'clock. On rainy days the trip would be cancelled.

We think that many of the first graders will want to take part in this activity. We could use some help transporting the children and giving them supervision. So if you have lived on a farm or have parents, grandparents, or great grandparents who have, we would like your help. Your child would like to work with mom and dad, too. If you have any questions, or if you could help with the garden project, call us at 222-0911.

If you want your child to have this opportunity please sign the form below and return it to the school.

I would like my child to stay after school on_____ afternoon to work in the first grade garden.

_____
Parent's Signature

REMINDER

March 12, 1965

Dear Parents:

This little note is to serve as a reminder to you and your child about the Civic Music Association Concert presented by the Paul Winter Jazz Sextet.

The children will be picked up at their homes between 7:30 and 8:00 P.M. on Sunday, March 14, 1965. They will be taken to Quincy Junior High School for the concert. The children will be returned to their home after intermission by the chaperone. They should arrive between 9:30 and 10:00 P.M.

Thank you for your cooperation.

SELF CONCEPT INSTRUMENT

School_____

Name_____

1.	Yes	No	I usually like to go to school.

1. Yes No   I usually like to go to school.
2. Yes No   I usually ask the teacher to explain something again if I don't understand.
3. Yes No   When school work is hard, I usually give up.
4. Yes No   I try to change when I know I'm doing things wrong.
5. Yes No   Doing well in my school work is important to me.
6. Yes No   I do my school work without being told more than once.
7. Yes No   I don't like to start work on new things.
8. Yes No   I often forget what the teacher told us to do next
9. Yes No   It is easy for me to stand up in front of the class and tell them something.
10. Yes No   I often do things without thinking.
11. Yes No   I get my work done on time.
12. Yes No   I sometimes copy from my friends.
13. Yes No   Fairly often I give up because I don't understand something.
14. Yes No   I often make mistakes because I didn't listen carefully.
15. Yes No   I try to be careful about my work.
16. Yes No   I get scared when I'm called on in class.
17. Yes No   I find it hard to remember things.
18. Yes No   I usually understand a story the first time I read it.
19. Yes No   I do well on tests.
20. Yes No   I feel good about my school work.
21. Yes No   Often I don't understand what is going on in class
22. Yes No   I don't have trouble learning.
23. Yes No   I solve problems quite easily.
24. Yes No   Most kids are smarter than I am.
25. Yes No   I often know the answer before the rest of the class.
26. Yes No   I can figure things out for myself.

27. Yes No   I get good grades easily.
28. Yes No   I find it easy to get along with my classmates.
29. Yes No,   I like the kids in this class very much.
30. Yes No   I try to play fair with my classmates.
31. Yes No   I am an important person to my classmates.
32. Yes No   My classmates like me.
33. Yes No   Most of my best friends are in this class.
34. Yes No   I find it hard to talk to classmates.
35. Yes No   I feel left out of things in class.
36. Yes No   My classmates miss me when I'm absent from school.

REPORT OF STUDENTS WORKING WITH CHILDREN IN QUINCY YOUTH DEVELOPMENT PROJECT

Your Name_____

Name of the children you work with and their ages_____
_____

Address of the children_____
_____

What school or schools do the children attend_____
_____

Date you worked with the children_____

Where did you go and what did you do?_____
_____
_____
_____

Did you talk to the parents—if so comment_____
_____

Did anyone help you? If so—Who_____
_____

Please add additional comments as to your observation of the children —Did they seem to enjoy themselves?—Do you think they learned anything?—How did they react to you, shy, aggressive, etc.? Did they say anything about themselves showing areas of need? Etc.

FIELD TRIP, THIRD GRADE—1964-65*

PLACE: City Dog Pound and Animal Hospital
OBJECTIVES:
    1. To provide vicarious experiences to develop a love and pro-

tection for animals in children.

2. To widen the child's knowledge of and sympathy for animals of all kinds.

3. To supplement the child's knowledge of textbook presented materials.

4. To provide a background experience to serve as a basis for vocabulary development.

5. To provide an enrichment experience to serve as a resource activity for written expression.

SUGGESTED PRE-TRIP ACTIVITIES:

Read and discuss Unit 4, "Animals in Town and Country," *The New Streets and Roads*, (Pages 166-192). Unit 3, "Desert Plants and Animals," (Pages 42-56) in *Science Far and Near*, will also increase the student's understanding of this field trip.

Use teacher guide for specific concepts and understandings which are to be developed.

Show audio-visual aids on animals.

The following films are available from the loan department of the Illinois State Museum.

Animal Homes, 11 minutes.

Animals Growing Up, 11 minutes.

Animals—Ways They Eat, 11 minutes.

Bear and Its Relatives, B.S., 22 minutes.

Dear and Its Relatives, B.W., 11 minutes.

Chucky Lou—Story of a Woodchuck, 11 minutes.

Little Animals, P., 11 minutes.

How Do You Zoo, P.B.W., 11 minutes.

Our Animal Neighbors P-I, 11 minutes.

Mississippi-Valley Libraries. Film Co-op.

Adventures of Willie Skunk, B.&W., 11 minutes.

#176 True Book of Animal's Babies. Filmstrip.

Quincy Public Schools

Animals Growing Up, 11 minutes.

Care of Pets, 10 minutes.

Gray Squirrel, 11 minutes.

Our Animal Neighbors, 11 minutes.

Shep, The Farm Dog, 11 minutes.

How Animals Defend Themselves, 11 minutes.

Animal Homes, 10 minutes.

Wonders in the Desert, 10 minutes.

#347 Farm Pets

#350 Farm Animals and Pets

#404 Deserts

#1643 Plant Life of the Desert

#1644 Desert Life

Wonders in the Desert, 10 minutes, Churchill-Wexler Film Productions.

Read and display stories and poems about animals. The following books are available at the Quincy Public Library to supplement your room libraries.

So You're Going to Get A Puppy, Col. S. P. Meek

Zoo Doctor, William Bridges

(Teacher may like to read one specific chapter to the class from this book)

First Aid to Animals, Boy Scouts of America.

There are many books available at the public library under this topic and these will be provided for you.

SUGGESTED POST-TRIP ACTIVITIES:

1. Teachers and pupils should discuss field trip. Encourage pupils to talk about things they learned at the Dog Pound and the Animal Hospital.

2. Keep classroom pet (such as mice, hamster, flying squirrel, or guinea pig) to show students that these animals are dependent upon them for food, shelter, etc. when they are kept in captivity.

3. Make bulletin board display of common-types of dogs and cats. Other bulletin boards might display home of animals, How To Care For Your Pet, or Common Pets In Our Area.

4. Write stories or poems for publication in parents newsletter.

5. Students will be taken to local dog shows and attend obedience training class in small groups. The Culver-Stockton students or Girl Scouts chaperone this activity.

°Quincy Youth Development Commission

BIBLIOGRAPHY

Liddle, Gordon P.: The school's job with the disaffected. *Educational Leadership,* February, 1963.

Liddle, Gordon P., and Rockwell, Robert E.: The role of parents and family life. *The Journal of Negro Education,* Summer 1964, reprinted in Fall 1964 issue.

Liddle, Gordon P., and Rockwell, Robert E.: The kid with two strikes against him. *Safety Education,* December, 1963.

Liddle Gordon P.: Modifying the school experience of culturally handicapped children in the primary grades. *Programs for the Educationally Disadvantaged,* USOE 35044, 1963. In somewhat different form this article appeared in *Today's Educational Programs for Culturally Deprived Children,* Division of School Psychologists, American Psychological Association, August, 1962 and in the *Illinois Journal of Education,* March, 1963.

Rockwell, Robert E.: Disadvantaged children and youth. *Illinois Clubwoman,* January, 1965.

Rockwell, Robert E.: A community resource. *Girl Scout Leader,* March, 1965.

Rockwell, Robert E.: Puppets for oral expression. *School Activities,* November, 1964.

Sacadat, Evelyn: Arousing parent interest in a program for the culturally deprived. *The Journal of Negro Education,* Spring 1965.

Sacadat, Evelyn, and Liddle, Gordon P.: Culturally disadvantaged. *Illinois Education,* November, 1965.

Sacadat, Evelyn: This way to the orchard. *School Activities,* March, 1964.

Sacadat, Evelyn, and Liddle, Gordon P.: Change has many facets. *Education,* Spring 1966.

Sacadat, Evelyn: Helping culturally handicapped children. *Educational Leadership,* April, 1965.

Sacadat, Evelyn: Head start makes a discovery. *Illinois Education,* January, 1967.

INDEX

A

Art enrichment, 28-30
 early experience in, 29
 art exhibits, 32, *See also* Art exhibits
 evaluation of program in, 29-30
 factors in teachers' lack of interest in, 28
 initiation of classes for, 28
 objectives of program, 28
 use exhibition to recognize children's abilities, 29
 use seasonal motif, 28-29
  use in classroom decoration, 29
 use of various art media, 29
Art exhibits, 32
 art workshop at Whitman School, 32
 availability of art shows through Art Club, 32
 purpose of, 32

B

Background and organization of project, 3-11
 community, 3-4, *See also* Community
 experimental design for program, 9-10, *See also* Experimental design
 factors in initiation of program, 4-5
  academic and social problems of High School graduates, 5
  evaluation first efforts with non-achieving secondary school students, 5
  initiation pilot program in primary grades at Whitman School, 5-6
  percentage of graduates of elementary schools finishing High School, 4

poor achievement in secondary schools following elementary school graduation, 4
  poor scholastic records of children from lower-class families, 4
 objectives of program, 6-7
 schools involved in program, 7
  facilities of, 7
 staff involved in program, 10-11
  professional staff time classification, table, 11
 teachers involved in program, 7-9
  factors in choice of types chosen for, 7-9
  training and environment of, 8-9
Bene-Anthony Family Relations Test, 70
Bowman, Paul, 4

C

California Test of Mental Maturity, 76
Camps, summer day, *See* Summer day camps
Civic Music Association, 31
Community, 3-11
 ethnic groups of, 3
 impact of program on, 96-98
  college students assistance in children's activities, 97
  dance program begun, 97
  Girl Scout assistance in children's activities, 98
  greater use of library facilities, 97-98
  initiation reading and study center, 97
  program as guide for Project Head Start, 96-97
 percent Negro population in, 3

109

children included in experimental group, 9
data recorded to determine types children helped by program, 10
division study program population, 9
   control group, 9
   experimental group, 9
use Metropolitan Reading Readiness Test, 10
use Peabody Picture Vocabulary Test, 9-10
use Primary Mental Abilities Test, 10
use Wechsler Intelligence Scale for Children, 9-10

F

Field trips, 19-23
   application of in class room, 20
      methods used, 20
   availability places for, 23
   basic objective of, 19
   choice of sites for, 20-21
   development skills of children through, 22
      arithmetic, 22
      map reading, 22
      thank-you letter writing, 22
   educational value of, 19-20
   example of one described, 22-23
   inclusion site of fathers' work, 22
   notice of, example, 103-105
   number trips conducted during four year program, 19
   planning for by program staff and parents, 21-22
      collection materials, 22
      supervision of, 21
      transportation, 21
   preparation for, 19-20
Fine Arts Society, 31

G

Garden project, 30-31
   class room application to, 31

family cooperation in, 31
   initiation of in second and third grades, 30
   note to parents for, example, 101
   percentage experimental group participating, 30
   factors in attendance slump during summer, 30-31
   procedure in preparing garden, 30
      by children, 30
      exchange of jobs, 30
      supervision, 30
      time involved, 30
      tools used, 30
   value of, 31

H

Havighurst, Robert J., v, 4, 5
Hess, Robert, 25
Hollister, William, v

I

Initial phase experiment, 12-18
   composition of advisory committee, 12
   initial comparison experimental and control groups, 17-18
      degree cultural handicap, table, 18
      initial intelligence test results, table, 17
      Metropolitan Test of Reading Readiness, table, 18
   initial home interviews, 15-17
      ambitions of parents for education of children learned, 16
      Church attendance rate of children, 16-17
      comparison education levels control and experimental group parents, 16
      home environment, 16
      percentage moderate handicapping parents, 16
      percentage parents in control group finishing High School, 15